ANALYSING DEMAND FOR RAIL TRAVEL

Analysing Demand for Rail Travel

Edited by

TONY FOWKES
CHRIS NASH

Avebury

ITS INSTITUTE FOR TRANSPORT STUDIES 4

Published by
Avebury
Academic Publishing Group
Gower House
Croft Road
Aldershot
Hants
GU11 3HR

Gower Publishing Company
Old Post Road
Brookfield
Vermont 05036
USA

A CIP catalogue record for this book is available from the British Library and the US Library of Congress.

ISBN 1 85628 136 1

Printed in Great Britain by
Athenaeum Press Ltd, Newcastle upon Tyne.

Contents

Series preface

The Institute for Transport Studies at the University of Leeds is the largest university transport research group in the U.K., and conducts research on a wide range of transport policy, planning and management issues. This series of monographs is designed to present results of this research in a greater depth that can be accommodated in journal articles, but to a wider audience than is reached by research reports to sponsors.

C. A. Nash
Professor of Transport Economics
Series Editor

List of contributors

Dr. Tony Fowkes, Institute for Transport Studies, University of Leeds

Dr. Eileen Hill, MVA Consultancy

Dr. Roger Mackett, Transport Studies Group, University College London

Phillipa Marks, National Economic Research Associates

Professor Chris Nash, Institute for Transport Studies, University of Leeds

Dr. John Preston, Institute for Transport Studies, University of Leeds

Dr. Julie Rickard, TPA Consultants

Dr. Mark Wardman, Institute for Transport Studies, University of Leeds

1 Introduction

CHRIS NASH

Rail transport no longer occupies the dominant position it once held in passenger transport. In Britain, it now accounts for only some 7% of domestic passenger kilometres travelled, with car (at 84%) the overwhelmingly dominant mode.

Yet these figures understate the importance of rail transport demand for two main reasons.

In the first place, rail remains an important mode of transport for specific markets and to significant groups of people. For instance, it still dominates commuting into London and business travel on the major inter city routes to London. Moreover, rail traffic in Britain has grown over the past decade, unlike bus traffic, which has continued to decline.

Secondly, rail transport is widely seen as a mode of transport the role of which will tend to increase, rather than decline, as congestion and environmental factors increasingly constrain the growth of car and air transport. Thus, throughout Europe, large scale investment is taking place both in high speed inter city rail routes and in urban and suburban systems. It has been estimated that the railways of Western Europe are likely to invest between £8 billion and £12 billion during the 1990's.

It is therefore a matter of some concern that relatively little has been published on the analysis of the demand for rail transport. This volume aims to fill that gap. At the same time, by explaining and illustrating a wide range of demand analysis methods, it aims to provide useful reading for all involved in analysing the demand for transport by whatever mode.

The exposition of the methodology is supplemented by references to empirical studies. In particular, we highlight work largely undertaken at the Institute for Transport Studies, University of Leeds. The chapter authors are all present or past members of staff of the Institute. Such a concentration of work has come about largely as the result of the sponsorship of two posts at the Institute by British Rail. We are grateful to British Rail for this sponsorship and to many members of British Rail staff for advice and encouragement, which made the major effort on rail demand analysis recorded in this book possible. We must also express our gratitude to Elizabeth Battye, who turned chapters written in a variety of manuscript and word processing systems into camera ready copy with her usual care and efficiency.

2 Needs, sources and methods

CHRIS NASH

2.1 Introduction

Compared with the vast literature on road traffic forecasting, the number of publications on the demand for rail travel is very limited. This should not be surprising. The provision of road space is the responsibility of public authorities, and most of the demand forecasting work undertaken by them or on their behalf is in the public domain. By contrast rail passenger undertakings, despite the fact that they are almost invariably publicly owned, are organised as separate commercial enterprises. In an increasingly competitive world, they are naturally circumspect about how much of their demand forecasting work they publish.

The needs of rail managers are also somewhat different from those of road planners. Only occasionally are they involved in long run forecasting exercises of a strategic nature, in which major infrastructure investment or routeing strategies are at stake. Most rail decisions are rather more incremental in nature. Most railways have a yearly (or twice yearly) timetable planning round, in which a host of detailed decisions regarding frequencies, exact timings, availability of through services and the like have to be taken for a period usually only starting many months into the future (the need to plan the allocation of resources to perform them means that on British Rail, for example, most decisions about the commercial specification of a timetable have to be taken at least nine months before it comes into force). Pricing decisions, similarly, are typically taken annually. Whilst the starting point may be a uniform increase in line with inflation, consideration has to be given not just to the overall real level of fares, but also to the case for selective increases or decreases on particular routes or for particular types of ticket. Even investment decisions may often be incremental rather than strategic - a particular track upgrading or the introduction of new or reallocated rolling stock may only save a few minutes on a particular journey, or the latter may give the passengers a more comfortable environment in which to travel.

Given this need for extensive knowledge on the short to medium term response of the market to modest changes in a host of variables, it is not surprising that the techniques in common use in rail transport rely heavily on simple elasticity models rather than the large scale comprehensive transport demand models of road transport. There is another important reason for this difference in emphasis. Surveys suggest that in any given year rather less than half the population of Great Britain makes any journeys by rail. For those who do make long distance rail trips, the mean number of return journeys made is only about one. Clearly any model which relies on random sampling of households for its calibration is going to require very large and expensive surveys to pick up an adequate number of rail users. This has led rail researchers to rely heavily on what can be done with existing data sources, such as ticket sales data, or by means of relatively cheaply undertaken on-train surveys. The result is a much better understanding of the preferences of existing rail travellers than of the reasons why the rest of the population choose not to travel by rail.

The aim of this chapter is to consider the needs, data sources and methods used in studying the demand for rail travel at the present time. It also provides a brief overview of the contents of later chapters. Although the methods used should be of general interest, the results given are confined to the position in Britain. Thus a few words about the institutional arrangements in Britain may be appropriate. Rail passenger transport in Britain, except for metros within a couple of the major cities and some short steam enthusiast's lines, is provided exclusively by British Rail, currently a publicly owned corporation, although there is much discussion of schemes for its privatisation. Whilst passenger services as a whole are subsidised, for many years now it has been the policy of successive governments that InterCity services should not be subsidised. In 1982, a clearly defined InterCity sector was created covering the principal trunk routes, with its own director and responsible for its own revenue, costs and assets. With effect from 1988 it ceased to be eligible for subsidy. In the case of other services (which have been grouped into Network South East, a sector covering London commuter services, and Regional Railways (formerly Provincial), which covers local and cross country services elsewhere in the country) subsidy is continuing but at a steadily reducing rate, and the priority of railway management is seen as being to improve the commercial performance of these services. Indeed, subsidy for Network South East is intended to cease in 1992/93. Thus, this book is written very much from the point of view of a commercially oriented railway. Nevertheless, the information requirements to fulfil almost any sensible alternative objectives would be very similar, even if the way the data would be used would be different.

The contents of this chapter are as follows. The next three sections give an overview of the need for forecasts, the data sources available and the alternative techniques to be found in the literature. Following that, we describe the areas of application dealt with in later chapters. Finally, we bring together some conclusions on the methods currently used by British Rail.

2.2   The need for forecasts

An organisation the size of British Rail requires demand forecasts at many levels of aggregation and for many purposes. At the strategic level, aggregate forecasts are required for long run planning over a timescale of twenty to thirty years. More detailed forecasts, but over a similar time span, are required for major investment projects such as electrification. Forecasting exercises looking this far ahead tend to be one-off studies tailored to a particular subject. By contrast the medium range - five to ten years ahead - is the subject of routine analysis in the annual corporate plan. Fares and services are generally revised annually, although more frequent adjustments are possible. In the case of fares, the starting point is to determine an overall level of increase for each of the three sectors of the passenger business - InterCity, Network South East and Regional Railways. Differential increases may then be decided upon for individual ticket types or for particular routes. Service planning also takes place on an annual cycle, although a major recast of the timetable for any particular route only occurs every few years; in the intervening years the process is more one of marginal adjustment. At this level of detail there is a need to be able to predict the short term effects of marginal changes in frequencies, speeds and the exact departure times of trains.

For short term forecasting, a knowledge of the various elasticities in question is generally adequate, since changes are typically marginal and the time period is such that many factors may reasonably be assumed constant. The full list of elasticities for which values are required is however formidable. A typical InterCity route has the following set of principle fares (numerous less common fares or special promotions also exist):

First Class Single and (Open) Return
Standard Class Single and (Open) Return
Super Saver Return (valid on days other than Fridays and summer
        Saturdays for return within a month, but excludes travel on
        key business trains)
Saver Return (as above, but valid on any day and on a greater
        range of trains)
Season tickets for various periods, usually related to each other by
        a simple formula.

The simple rule for profit maximisation is to raise any fare where the price elasticity is less than one, at least until the elasticity reaches one, and beyond provided that the cost savings from the resulting loss of traffic offset the revenue reduction involved. (In practice, this is unlikely to be the case for a rail service unless the frequency of service is reduced as well, requiring a further estimate of the traffic loss this involves). Clearly this requires one to estimate a separate elasticity for each of the five ticket types and a knowledge of how this elasticity varies as fares change.

But this rule ignores the important phenomenon of revenue abstraction. To explain what this is and why it is so important, a simple example may help. Suppose that the elasticity for Saver fares is estimated at -1.5. A ten per cent cut in fares would be expected to yield a fifteen per cent increase in traffic and a three and a half per cent increase in revenue. However, suppose that just two out of every fifteen passengers attracted to buy Saver tickets by this lower fare have diverted from Standard tickets at twice the price. This degree of abstraction (which is quite consistent with a cross price elasticity of demand for standard tickets with respect to Saver fares as low as 0.2) would completely offset the revenue advantage of the fares reduction. With five ticket types, the total number of potential cross price elasticities to be estimated is twenty, although many of these may reasonably be expected to be negligible.

6

We have talked so far of identifying separate elasticities by ticket type, as these correspond to the various products the railway has on offer. But a far more natural way of disaggregating the market is by market segment in terms of journey purpose and person type. The relationship between the two is, of course, determined by the mix of purpose and person types to be found on each ticket type. There is no easy mapping of one into the other. For instance, although most first class travel is travel in the course of work, a greater amount of travel for this purpose is to be found in the standard class. Obviously, elasticities for individual ticket types can be estimated from those for journey purpose if the proportion of travel for each journey purpose by ticket type is known. If it is postulated that the underlying elasticities by purpose are the same across all routes, then this also holds out the prospect of economically estimating separate elasticities by route from the different proportions of holders of each ticket type travelling for each purpose on each route. However, in reality, elasticities by route will vary with the alternatives available for travel on each route. Furthermore, it is likely that travellers for a particular purpose who choose a cheaper fare are, on average, more price sensitive than those who travel on a more expensive one; for instance businessmen who travel standard class are likely to be more price sensitive than those who travel first. Thus a knowledge of elasticities by journey purpose is really no substitute for a knowledge by ticket type.

Estimation of elasticities with respect to service quality may appear more straightforward. In fact, the reverse is the case. There is as great a range of possible service quality variables as there is types of ticket. Many of these variables have no natural units of measurement. Even the measurement of journey time and frequency is problematic (do all trains count or only the fast ones? Do trains in the early hours of the morning count equally with those in the late afternoon peak?). Other variables such as comfortable seating, a pleasant environment and helpful staff are far more difficult to measure. To estimate the revenue effect of an improvement in service level, one needs again to disaggregate by ticket type. There is even an effect analogous to the cross price effect in price elasticities. Selective improvement of the service available to holders of only some types of ticket may abstract traffic from other ticket types. For instance, this may happen when the quality of the catering in the first class is improved, or new first class only services are introduced.

In Britain, an important quality of service issue is that of changes in the set of trains on which the cheaper tickets are available. For instance, a train in the shoulder of the morning or evening peak may have spare capacity, and opening it up to users of Saver tickets may significantly increase the attractiveness of the product. But if a substantial number of existing business travellers switch to the cheaper ticket, there will be an important loss of revenue to take into account.

By this stage, the number of different elasticities we may be interested in may easily have reached forty or fifty. The impossibility of ever estimating such a large number of effects may well incline the reader to rely on managerial judgement backed up by the monitoring of systematic experimentation. Even this has its limitations, however, as it is seldom possible to hold controlled experiments in which only one variable is varied at a time, and therefore without a model it is often impossible to disentangle cause and effect, particularly given the difficulties in obtaining reliable data to be discussed below.

As we look further ahead in time, the problem becomes simpler in some senses but more complex in others. On the one hand, the extent to which we need to worry about the fine detail of fares structure and service level tends to diminish - more broad averaging becomes acceptable. But on the other hand the range of variables in which we are concerned increases. Significant changes in the size and distribution of the population become possible; the mix of age, household structure and socio-economic groups changes and major developments in the quality of the competition may emerge. If the railway is considering entering new markets, or markets in which it currently has a very minor share - for instance, by a rerouteing strategy or by a new quality product - then the application of elasticities to a base load traffic (even with allowance for how the elasticities may change as fares or service levels change) may not be adequate. In such cases the volume of traffic must be estimated from scratch.

2.3   Data sources

Ticket sales

Where elasticity information is really all that is needed, the most obvious approach to the problem is to rely on cross section or time series analysis of ticket sales data. Inevitable in the use of ticket sales data are the problems that:

8

1. At best, the data only gives the originating and terminating station of the rail portion of the journey. If feeder journeys are made by other modes, these do not correspond to the true origin and destination.

2. In practice, there are many circumstances in which through tickets are not issued, or in which it is advantageous to rebook en route to take advantage of cheaper fares. In this case, even the rail origin and destination are incorrectly recorded. Moreover, changes in fare structure and ticketing arrangements over time mean that this distortion is not a constant percentage of sales on a particular route. For instance, introduction of a new bargain ticket between Liverpool and London in 1981 was accompanied by a massive increase in sales, only part of which was genuinely new business. The rest consisted of passengers making journeys passing through Liverpool and London who now found it worthwhile to rebook at those points.

3. Ticket sales data cannot reveal the day or time at which the journey was made (important issues in the matching of supply and demand), nor even whether the ticket was used at all. These issues are most important in the case of season tickets, where the journeys being purchased are spread over a period of up to a year, and where premature surrender or renewal of the ticket is quite common, particularly when fare increases are pending.

4. Ticket sales data reveals nothing of the use made of travelcards or system passes such as have become popular in metropolitan areas under the instigation of the Passenger Transport Executives.

In addition to this, until recently there were a number of particular problems with the ticket sales data held by British Rail.

5. A large proportion of tickets sold were not allocated to particular routes (the so-called 'blanks' problem). On InterCity routes, these typically comprised some thirty per cent of total traffic. Wherever printed tickets were used, stocks were only held of the more commonly used tickets. Other tickets were handwritten, and full details of these did not enter the system. Some sorts of ticket machine, including all those used by guards to issue tickets on trains, did not record information on origins and destinations. Tickets sold at travel agents were particularly likely to be handwritten. Again, there was not even consistency over

time, in that the variety of printed tickets held would be varied in accordance with the demand. Thus the coverage of the system could vary over time.

6. The system was prone to data errors or the absence of complete batches of data, due either to human error or machine failure. Again, this was not just a random error; as a particular batch of ticket machines aged and became less reliable, so the proportion of data captured at those sales points would decline over time.

7. The data was not held in a form which lent itself readily to time series comparisons. For the most part, managers received the information in the form of hard copy referring to a particular time period.

Many of these problems have been overcome by the new 'state of the art' information system now being introduced. A new set of computer programmes, known as CAPRI (computer analysis of passenger receipts and information), provides a more flexible source of information on line. It receives information nightly over the telephone line from a new generation of ticket machine that stores full details of all tickets sold. A portable version of this machine is available for use on train and at less busy locations. Because the new machines are able to issue a much greater variety of tickets than those they replace, the problem of handwritten tickets is very much reduced. Some problems remain (eg. with travel agents not fully connected to the new system, or with incorrect on-train recording of origins and destinations in areas where virtual 'flat fare' schemes operate off-peak) but the position is much improved. However, it is not easy to provide a long time series from CAPRI by linking it to earlier data sources, and year on year comparisons have thus become more popular.

Thus the particular problems of the previous British Rail system should be overcome in the next few years. However, the work discussed below was all undertaken at a time when CAPRI data was unavailable. In any event, any time series work on ticket sales data will still have to rely on the pre-CAPRI data for many years, until an adequate run of better data is available. Indeed, initially the new system hampered rather than aided time series analysis, as there was a gradual improvement in the quality and coverage of the data over a number of years, making the more recent data increasingly inconsistent with the earlier data.

Passenger counts

A further source of data which is collected on a routine basis is the number of passengers on each main line train at several points on its journey. This information is collected by the guard, and at least partly fills the gap in knowledge as to the exact distribution of passengers between trains. For local services "on-off" counts are undertaken periodically at stations, with the same purpose in mind. However, there is no very reliable way of estimating passenger origins and destinations from this source and it has only recently been computerised. Thus it has been very little used in demand analysis.

Survey analysis

We have already commented on the difficulty of obtaining adequate samples for household surveys of long distance travel by all modes. Where fresh surveys have to be undertaken, it is very much simpler to interview rail passengers than to obtain a cross section of users of all modes. On long distance trains, there is time to undertake interviews, or to distribute a self completion questionnaire for completion on the spot. Response rates little short of 100 per cent are typically achieved. British Rail has always undertaken occasional 'profile' surveys of passengers for particular purposes, and now has continuous surveys providing information on the characteristics and attitudes of passengers (the Monitors). No doubt it was partly the ease of undertaking such surveys which encouraged British Rail to try to push the information on preferences acquired in this way further by the use of the 'Stated Preference' techniques discussed below. Surveying on other modes of transport is more problematic - for instance it is difficult to intercept inter city car travellers en route. Thus surveys covering all modes of transport tend to be undertaken at home. This is more costly, and typically achieves response rates of the order of 30%, with a bias towards those particularly interested in the purpose of the questionnaire.

2.4   Types of model

The traditional approach to transport demand forecasting in urban areas is the aggregate sequential model, which considers in turn the number of trips generated by and attracted to each zone, the distribution of trips between zones, mode split and assignment (or choice of route). Each of these stages is represented by an equation estimated usually on aggregate data. We have commented above on the expense and difficulty of obtaining the necessary data to estimate such a model for long distance travel by all modes. There is also a further problem. Market research suggests that when rail services or fares are changed, a considerable proportion of the resulting change in volume represents not people who have switched modes or destinations but trips which have been newly generated or suppressed. It would be difficult to model this adequately in the trip generation equations of a model which would inevitably be dominated by car travel; in any event most models of this type do not allow for elastic trip generation at all. Thus there may be theoretical as well as pragmatic reasons to prefer the single mode direct demand models which have usually been used in practice in this field. The one example of a model of the above structure being applied to InterCity travel of which we are aware reveals the problems described above. This is the study carried on a European scale by OECD (1977).

From the first, demand forecasting work within British Rail has relied on direct demand models. The first model (Tyler and Hassard, 1973) of this sort to be calibrated on ticket sales data was the model MONICA (Model for Optimising the Network of Inter City Activities). This initially used cross section data for sixty-four flows to and from London. The main aim of the work was to identify the effect of speed on traffic volumes, in order to evaluate investments designed to permit higher speeds. A particular problem in cross section analysis is that journey time, price and distance are all highly correlated. This problem was circumvented in this case by introducing the variables 'price' and 'speed' into the model, recognising that this would lead to a bias in the price elasticity coefficient, which would pick up all of the effect of distance, but hoping for an unbiased coefficient on speed.

Also of interest is the particular measure of speed adopted in this study, which actually combined the effects of speed and frequency, and has remained as the principal measure of service quality in subsequent British Rail work. We have already commented on the difficulty in measuring both speed and frequency for a service which contains a mixture of fast and slow trains. For instance, if a simple average speed is used then the addition of more slow trains will reduce its value, although they may actually enhance the timetable by filling gaps in the service. If average speed and frequency are used as two separate variables, they will still fail to account for issues such as the way in which trains are spaced out through the day, whilst a moderate average

12

speed in which all trains take the same time may generate very different traffic levels to the same average but with half the trains being very fast and the other half slow. The solution to this dilemma which Tyler and Hassard used was to ask the question 'suppose that passengers' desired departure (or arrival) times were evenly spread throughout an x hour day. What would be the average length of time from their desired departure time until they could reach their destination, proceeding by the next available train (obviously any slow trains that would be overtaken in the course of their journey would be ignored)'. For even-interval services this would of course be simply the journey time plus half the headway. Subsequent work has improved on the original formulation by incorporating peaks in demand. The way in which this is done is to weight the journey time by the proportion of passengers wishing to depart at that time. Also, the costs involved in arriving at an earlier or later than ideal time have been more accurately valued.

At the time, the MONICA model represented a major step forward. Moreover some confirmatory evidence was provided by a Before and After study of the West Coast Main Line electrification, which estimated a journey time elasticity of 1.4 (Evans, 1969). This was exactly what MONICA would predict for a service with an average speed of sixty miles per hour (including waiting time). However, when subsequent services were accelerated, it appeared that the effect on traffic volume was substantially below that predicted by MONICA. The reason may have been partly that, as is usual with cross section models, the elasticities produced were very much long term ones. But the problem was also due to a difficulty with ticket sales data discussed above. Where a station had a particularly good service, its catchment area would be expanded at the expense of its inferior neighbours. Since the true origin of the trips was not known, this was ascribed to an increase in trip rates per head of population, rather than a redistribution of trips between origins (Shilton, 1982). Also, there may have been a problem of simultaneity bias, high traffic levels tending to lead to high quality services as well as the reverse.

Within British Rail, subsequent work on the effects of service accelerations utilised the control flow technique. This relied on finding a flow that had behaved similarly over time to the flow in question but which was not subject to acceleration, and ascribing the difference in behaviour of the two flows after the event to the service improvement. This suggested an elasticity with respect to journey time of the order of 0.8, but with some evidence that a smaller figure might apply to minor accelerations unaccompanied by a major marketing effort.

13

A further important development should be mentioned in the way in which such results were used. Acceleration of a particular train service does not just increase traffic flows between the origins and destinations served by the service in question. Many other flows of traffic would use the service for part of a journey involving interchange. A computer model was therefore built which divided the country into zones and calculated the improvement in service quality between each pair of zones produced by a given service acceleration. The appropriate elasticities would then be applied to a complete matrix of trips between these zones. This model, named MOIRA, has now been in use for many years for the examination of timetable changes. It forms a framework within which emerging evidence on elasticities from other sources may be utilised (Whitehead, 1981).

At the time of the development of MONICA, there was insufficient data available to permit calibration of the model to be by means of time series rather than cross section data. By the second half of the 1970's, however, this had changed, and the first published time series study of British Inter City rail traffic using ticket sales data was undertaken within the Department of Transport (Jones and Nichols, 1983). Data for seventeen routes was analysed over a period of seven years. Elasticities were estimated with respect to price, journey time, economic indicators and the level of competition (represented by dummy variables for such events as motorway openings). No significant frequency elasticity was found.

Further time series regression analysis of ticket sales data has been undertaken since (Fowkes, Nash and Whiteing, 1985; Owen and Phillips, 1987) and is discussed in chapter 3; it is clearly a very important approach, not just for obtaining an overall view of average price and journey time elasticities, but also for examining underlying trends in demand, the effect of car ownership growth and the state of the economy. But it is clear that there are important questions which this type of analysis is unlikely to be able to answer. Quality of service variables are often highly correlated with each other, and disentangling the effects of variables such as speed, frequency and the need to change trains is not easy, particularly when some of the variables only exhibit very modest variability, and the underlying data source contains a great deal of inaccuracy. It is difficult to obtain adequate information even by ticket type, given the number of cross elasticities that then have to be estimated; breaking down by journey purpose or person type with ticket sales data is not possible. For this reason, British Rail pioneered the use in the transport field in this country of modern Stated Preference

14

techniques, in a study by Sheldon and Steer (1982). The essence of these techniques is that respondents are asked to rank, rate, or choose between hypothetical alternatives in which improvement in one attribute can only be had at the expense of a worsenment in another. Variants of this technique have been extensively used and we discussed, along with other disaggregate methods, in chapter 4.

2.5   Areas of application

Chapters 5 to 9 of the book switch from considering methods in general to examining experience in a number of specific areas of application. Chapter 5 discusses the results of two studies of the preferences of leisure travellers. It shows how Stated Preference techniques may be used to obtain disaggregated information for particular types of travellers, and how they can be used to value attributes such as departure time or time spent standing, which it is difficult to address with aggregate econometric methods.

Chapter 6 turns to business travel. This is particularly difficult to analyse because of the mix of organisation and individual preferences revealed by a study of actual travel behaviour. It is found that both employers and employees place very high values on travel time savings when undertaking long distance business trips.

Commuting journeys also present difficulties, in that simple elasticity type models ignore the fact that if more people commute in one corridor then - unless home and job locations have changed - fewer must commute in another. Chapter 7 presents two models - one aggregate and one disaggregate - which take account of this effect and suggest that simple models may be quite misleading, at any rate in London where rail dominates the market.

Another context in which simple elasticity models are of little use is where one is trying to forecast demand for a station or service that does not currently exist. In chapter 8, a range of models is considered to address this problem; it is concluded that the appropriate approach depends on the scale of the investment and on whether the investment is being appraised on purely financial criteria or by social cost benefit appraisal (requiring knowledge of the level of diversion of traffic from other modes).

Finally, in chapter 9, the issues of socio economic and demographic change are addressed. Yet another different type of model is used here, akin to the 'category analysis' model of trip generation (Wootton and Pick, 1967) but estimated by Poisson regression techniques. In chapter 10 our conclusions, and suggestions for future work, are put forward.

2.6   Conclusion

The development of rail demand forecasting in Great Britain has been heavily conditioned by the availability of adequate data, and of the long list of needs outlined in the first part of this paper. Only a few of the most important can be said to be fully satisfied by the information currently available. Nevertheless it is now possible to see a well thought out, if pragmatic, approach to demand forecasting emerging within British Rail. This rests on time series analysis of ticket sales data for broad evidence on elasticities and longer term trends, supplemented by the use of Stated Preference techniques when more detailed knowledge of the effects of particular service changes or of elasticities at a very disaggregate level are required.   This approach serves well both for the examination of the short term effects of detailed changes in fares and services, and for longer term strategic studies. It is less helpful in the examination of new infrastructure, stations and services, where a number of techniques have been tried, but their relative reliability remains somewhat untested, and in looking at long term demographic and socio economic change.   Given the interest in these fields at the present time, development of appropriate techniques for these circumstances is now a high priority.

3 The aggregate approach

TONY FOWKES AND CHRIS NASH

3.1 Introduction

Railways, like other businesses, keep data on their levels of output, not only in terms of volume produced, but also volume sold and revenue received. British Rail, for instance, keep such data in four weekly period form. This then forms an obvious and cheap source of data for the application of aggregate econometric methods to rail demand analysis. This chapter will first give a simple overview of the methods used in the analysis of time series ticket sales data, and then consider the evidence available from studies of this type.

3.2 Model forms

The econometric method proceeds by relating a variable of interest (the dependent variable) to explanatory variables by some functional form, the parameters of which are to be estimated together with a measure of dispersion around the average value given by this function. We shall start by considering what 'variables' will be involved. Let us suppose that our dependent variable of interest is the number of rail journeys made between two cities. We can call this variable J, possibly with subscript t to indicate that it varies over time.

We now turn to consider what 'explanatory variables' we might use to explain the behaviour of J over time. The first that comes to mind is the fare, which we may denote F_t. This may be obtained by consulting fare manuals for all the relevant time periods, but this is often difficult since such data may not be easily available, fare changes may occur in the middle of time periods, and some sales may be at discounted fares for some reason (e.g. if bought with a railcard). Consequently, it is more common to use average revenue in place of the fare. Average revenue can be easily obtained by dividing revenue figures by the number of journeys, both these figures being commonly recorded. The major difficulty of using average revenue in place of fare comes when combining different ticket types. In that case a fall in average revenue may either reflect a fall in fares or reflect a movement from more expensive tickets to cheaper tickets. If the latter is common, the importance of fare in determining demand (journeys) will be misestimated.

A second group of explanatory variables relate to the service quality offered by the railway. There could be many possible indicators of service quality, but few are usually recorded or can be easily constructed. One important component of service quality is the rail journey time. Even if this is not stored, it is usually possible to reconstruct it from timetables. Closely related is the number of interchanges required, since these may be a severe disincentive to travel, and any time involved may be weighted more highly than for 'ordinary' journey time. A further component of the overall journey time is the access/egress time at each end of the rail journey. This can usually be safely neglected in time series work since stations do not 'move about' much. Exceptions are towns with two or more stations where service changes may alter which station is best for a particular journey, recent examples occurring in Bradford and Manchester, and cases where local road or public transport improvements significantly affect access/egress. Lastly the 'frequency' with which trains operate is important and is usually easily available.

Another 'time related' aspect of rail service quality is timetable achievement, i.e. having related demand to how good the timetable says the service is, we must now consider whether the timetable promise is delivered. From the operator's viewpoint there are two dimensions of failure; unpunctuality and unreliability/ cancellations. From the customer's point of view the distinction can become blurred. For instance, with a service having a half hourly frequency if all trains run 30 minutes late the service will appear perfect to users. If half of the trains alternately run to time and run 30 minutes late (possibly due to alternate trains having different starting points) then the frequency will appear to have fallen to hourly even though no trains have been cancelled. The same result, from the passenger's viewpoint, would have been achieved if alternate trains had been cancelled.

Turning to non time-related aspects of service quality we have the following:

- a quality of rolling stock effect
  (comfort/riding/cleanliness/availability of toilets, phones, etc.)
- a quality of station effect
  (ticketing arrangements/waiting facilities/availability of refreshments, shops, toilets, phones, lockers etc.)
- a quality of rail staff effect
  (is the station staffed?/are there staff on the train?/are they helpful? etc.)

Clearly, time series data on the above aspects are rarely collected, principally because they are so difficult to measure on any sort of consistent basis. Even a cross section study would face great difficulties.

A third group of explanatory variables relates to the service quality offered by other modes of transport (e.g. air, bus, car etc.). This quickly multiplies the number of variables that might be considered in our model, although data difficulties will exclude many. If a rail operator is conducting a study of their demand they may find it difficult to obtain similar data for competing bus because of commercial confidentiality. Air traffic data is more readily available, being collected at airports and published by the Civil Aviation Authority. With car the position is very difficult, very little data being collected by anyone for interurban travel. Even when funding is available, origin and destination surveys for car travel are limited by police restrictions on the choice of survey sites. Stopping cars for surveys on motorways, for example, is virtually banned. Costs of travel clearly vary with the speed the car travels and the type and condition of the car. These costs then have to be split amongst the occupants of the car, so it will be appreciated that wide variations in car per person costs, for a given journey, can occur quite apart from the well known cost reporting difficulties.

A fourth group of explanatory variables relate to factors outside of the transport sector. Clearly the amount of rail travel between two towns will be influenced by the size of the populations of the two towns and the economic conditions obtaining there. Trip rates per person can be expected to vary by sex, age, income, socio-economic group, level of car ownership etc.; probably with complex interactions. Since suitably disaggregated population data is unlikely to be available, only the more major effects can be allowed for. Often, economic well-being on the route is proxied by national measures such as gross domestic product (GDP). More localised data will be available for employment and registered unemployment. There is often a trade off between frequency of publication of data and the degree of disaggregation. For example, many data items at a county level are only available annually, whilst the same data items may be available monthly or quarterly at the national level.

Where socio-economic effects are changing only very slowly, e.g. the proportion of women in the population of a given town, they will be impossible to disentangle from other trend-related variables in an econometric investigation using time series data. The usual response of the econometrician is to include a time trend term to take account of the combined effect over time of all effects not explicitly considered. This is clearly a gross simplification and estimated coefficients of trend terms require careful and humble interpretation. Problems can easily arise when other included explanatory variables happen to have a strong trend-like element.

Besides measurable variables, demand studies make extensive use of the dummy variable. This comes in several forms in order to do different 'jobs'. For example, if we have quarterly data and wish to detect a fixed seasonal effect, dummy variables can be included for three of the four quarters. These dummy variables will take the value one during their quarter (each year) and zero otherwise. The quarter without a dummy variable becomes the base, with the estimated coefficients of the dummies for the other quarters each showing the average difference in traffic in that quarter relative to the base quarter. If a dummy variable has the value one in one period only, and is zero for all other periods, the effect is to prevent that period's data from having any influence on the model. This is particularly useful when a period's data has been completely distorted by a factor such as a strike. Dummy variables can be used to split the data series into two or more parts, and can be multiplied by any other variable so that, for example, separate fare effects can be estimated before and after some period in time.

Now that we have our variable of interest, JOURNEYS (J), and a host of potential explanatory variables, we need to consider how the former may be related to the latter. This is done mathematically, with the general form being called a function, i.e.

$$J = f \text{ (EXPLANATORY VARIABLES)}$$

The next step for an econometrician is to say that no functional form is likely to fit exactly (unless there are as many explanatory variables as there are observation points), so that we should include an 'error term'. This will give us what we term a 'model'. In a model it is customary for econometricians to denote all the unknowns by Greek letters. Since the errors are unknown let us denote them as ε_t, i.e. one for each time period t. Then we have

$$J_t = f \text{ (EXPLANATORY VARIABLES)} + \varepsilon_t$$

We shall first deal with the simple case where all the explanatory variables also relate to time period t, but in general this need not be the case. As we shall see, it is often the case that effects are lagged. This is particularly useful for forecasting purposes since this removes the need to forecast the explanatory variables to provide inputs to the model so as to predict JOURNEYS. To start with, though, let us assume that the explanatory variables relate to the same time period, t, as JOURNEYS. In this case the simplest model form is

$$Y_t = \alpha + \beta X_t + \varepsilon_t$$

In the above model, Y_t is the 'dependent' variable the behaviour of which is being explained by the simple explanatory variable X_t. α and β are 'parameters' of the model functional form which are to be estimated. If we have chosen a functional form which correctly models the actual situation, then α and β can be taken to be the 'true' values. They will remain unknown, but if we have time series data for Y_t and X_t we will be able to derive estimates of α and β, which we conventionally denote as $\hat{\alpha}$ and $\hat{\beta}$, i.e. we denote estimates by the symbol for the parameter they are estimating, with a 'hat' on. If the estimates are derived by statistical means the estimates are called 'statistics'. The estimation process will also produce further statistics, based on the residual variation after fitting the model, which show how well the model fits. We shall return to this later.

The form of the model shown above is called 'linear additive': linear because there are no squared or higher powers present; and additive because the model is constructed by addition. Hence to form a linear additive model with two explanatory variables (say X_1 and X_2) we would have

$$Y_t = \beta_0 + \beta_1 X_{1t} + \beta_2 X_{2t} + \varepsilon_t$$

and so on for any additional explanatory variables to be included. Such models are usually calibrated by linear regression, which merely chooses those values for β_0, β_1, β_2 etc. which minimise the squared residuals between observed and modelled values of Y_t. If we denote the modelled value of Y_t as $\hat{Y}_t$, we have (for the above case)

$$\text{MIN } \Sigma_t \, (Y_t - \hat{Y}_t)^2$$

i.e. $\quad \text{MIN } \Sigma_t \, (Y_t - \beta_0 - \beta_1 X_{1t} - \beta_2 X_{2t})^2$

For the case of only one explanatory variable, simple formulae can be written down for $\hat{\alpha}$ and $\hat{\beta}$, but for more than one explanatory variable (i.e. multiple regression) it is best to treat the estimation as a 'black box' and leave it to a computer package.

Least squares regression can handle a variety of model forms, not all of which would normally be regarded as 'linear', although usage of that word varies. For example we might include powers of explanatory variables, although this requires care and is rarely of use in rail ticket sales analysis. However, 'interaction terms' formed by the product of explanatory variables can be useful, as already mentioned in the case of dummy variables used to permit the effect of a given explanatory variable to vary, e.g.

$$J_t = \beta_0 + \beta_1 F_t + \beta_2 F_t D_t + \varepsilon_t$$

where J is JOURNEYS, F is FARE, and D is a dummy variable taking the value 1 in the summer and zero elsewhere. This model allows for the effect of fare on journeys made to be different in summer (when there are more leisure trips) than in winter (when price insensitive business travellers are more in evidence). The above model can be estimated by least squares regression directly without any difficulty.

Least squares can also be used for more complicated model forms after 'linearisation'. The most useful case here is of the multiplicative form, e.g.

$$Y_t = \beta_0 \, X_{1t}^{\beta_1} \, X_{2t}^{\beta_2} \varepsilon_t$$

Such forms can be linearised by taking logs, here giving

$$\log Y_t = \log \beta_0 + \beta_1 \log X_{1t} + \beta_2 \log X_{2t} + \log \varepsilon_t$$

If we relabel $\log Y_t$ as Y_t^*, $\log \beta_0$ as β_0^*, $\log X_{1t}$ as X_{1t}^*, $\log X_{2t}$ as X_{2t}^* and $\log \varepsilon_t$ as ε_t^*, then we can see we have a familiar equation form

$$Y_t^* = \beta_0^* + \beta_1 X_{1t}^* + \beta_2 X_{2t}^* + \varepsilon_t^*$$

This is suitable for least squares regression. For more complicated models that cannot be linearised we have to use different estimation techniques, usually based on maximum likelihood principles, which choose those parameter estimates which make the observed data most likely to have occurred. We are forced to make assumptions about the distribution of the error terms. These are sensibly usually assumed to have mean zero. The usual assumption as to shape is to assume a Normal distribution (a symmetrical bell shape around mean zero). In this case the maximum likelihood technique for linear regression is least squares estimation (as discussed above) with an estimate of the size of the variance (relating to the width of the bell) provided automatically. When the ε_t's cannot be assumed independent Normally distributed with mean zero, then ordinary least squares estimation will be inappropriate.

When we have several candidate models for consideration, we need some way (or ways) of judging which is best. Where the dependent variable does not vary between models there are agreed ways of how this should be done. One obvious criterion is how well the variation in the dependent variable has been explained by the explanatory variables. Expressed as a percentage this is denoted R^2, i.e.

R^2 = EXPLAINED SUM OF SQUARES/TOTAL SUM OF SQUARES

Clearly a model with higher R^2 is better than one with a lower R^2, all else equal. However, even a really useless explanatory variable will add something to R^2, and so will appear to improve the model. What we need to know is whether R^2 has improved sufficiently to make the inclusion of the extra variable worthwhile. We can do this by using a measure called the 'adjusted R^2', denoted $\overline{R}^2$, which will only increase if the extra variable adds more to the explained sum of squares than it takes away from the precision of the estimate of the error variance.

Much the same result is obtained by considering the t statistics of individual coefficients in the model. Where these are not significantly different from zero, the statistical estimation will be improved by their removal and $\overline{R}^2$ should increase. Sometimes, however, it is desirable to retain one or more non-significant variables in the model. This is because there are two reasons for obtaining non-significant coefficients: firstly because this explanatory variable has no effect on the dependent variable; and secondly because the size of the effect is too small to overcome the random effects. This second effect would be overcome with a big enough sample size, but econometric studies of such things as ticket sales data are generally very limited in length. Consequently where *a priori* economic reasoning suggests that a particular explanatory variable should have an effect, albeit possibly small, then it may be sensible to retain it in the equation even if its coefficient is non-significant, provided it has the correct sign.

A major problem with econometric time series work is multicollinearity, which is the name given to the situation where two or more explanatory variables are themselves closely correlated with each other. The reason why this tends to occur with time series data in particular is that many time series change only very gradually over time, perhaps increasing - perhaps decreasing, and so can be well represented by a simple linear model

$$X_{1t} = \alpha + \beta X_{2t}$$

where β will be negative if the series are going in opposite directions. Other time series variables are correlated because they each reflect some underlying behaviour, such as general economic well-being. In prosperous times national GDP will grow, numbers in employment will grow, unemployment will fall, earnings will grow etc.; all being reversed in less prosperous times. If general economic well-being has a large effect on each of the two series then they are likely to be correlated.

The problem caused by the presence of excessive multicollinearity is that the 'black box' cannot decide which of two collinear explanatory variables is having the effect on the dependent variable. If our only purpose is to forecast the dependent variable then there is no problem provided our forecast has the two collinear explanatory variables maintaining their past relationship with one another. However, more often we will wish to use the coefficient estimates themselves, e.g. to form demand elasticities with respect to the explanatory variables in question. In that case we could easily be misled if we used the estimated coefficients.

A second econometric problem with which we must deal is called autocorrelation, and refers to the situation where the error term at time t is related to the error at time t-1, or some earlier errors. Thus if hot weather increases trips by bringing out holiday makers, then during a warm spell each day's traffic would be above that expected, while during bad spells of weather traffic would be lower. Thus the deviation of actual ticket sales from expected ticket sales can be guessed at by knowing the deviation for the previous day. What we really have here is a case of a 'missing variable', since if a 'weather' variable were included in the model the problem would probably disappear. In general, we have to assume that all omitted variables have only very minor influences on the dependent variable, so that the combined effects of a multitude of omitted variables turns out to look like random 'white noise'.

If it is not possible to overcome autocorrelation by including a 'missing variable' then some form of transformation may be required. This can usually be thought of as making an adjustment for some lagged effect. A particularly popular and useful example is the partial adjustment model, which says that not all of the effect of the explanatory variables on the dependent variable takes place in the current period, but that the dependent variable is constantly partially adjusting to the changes in the explanatory variables. It is usually helpful to think of a basic model relating the DESIRED level of Y_t to explanatory variables $X_1 \ldots X_n$, with a separate equation relating the ACTUAL level of Y_t to its DESIRED level, say Y_t^*.

e.g. $Y_t^* = \beta_0 + \beta_1 X_{1t} + \beta_2 X_{2t} + \ldots + \beta_n X_{nt} + \varepsilon_t$

$Y_t = Y_{t-1} + \lambda (Y_t^* - Y_{t-1})$

Combining these equations gives

$Y_t = (1 - \lambda) Y_{t-1} + \lambda\beta_0 + \lambda\beta_1 X_{1t} + \lambda\beta_2 X_{2t} + \ldots + \lambda\beta_n X_{nt} + \varepsilon_t$

From the above it will be seen that such a model may be estimated simply by adding a lagged Y term to the right hand side of the model equation. The effect is equivalent to including exponentially decreasing effects for each variable over time. If the cause of the autocorrelation was the fact that changes in explanatory variables were continuing to have effects over several periods, then the partial adjustment model should remove the problem. The inclusion of the Y_{t-1} term, or lagged endogenous variable - as it is technically known - creates some more problems which need some care in handling. The first is care in interpreting the coefficients since a reliable estimate of λ must first be obtained if the $\lambda\beta$ estimates are to be divided to obtain the desired estimates of β. Secondly, the presence of the lagged endogenous variable

25

invalidates the usual test for autocorrelation, the Durbin Watson test, at least in its usual form.

Partial adjustment models are likely to be most relevant when the length of the time period is short, e.g. monthly data. When using annual data, on the other hand, it is much more likely that effects will be confined to the year in question. However, distributed lags are not the only sort that might be considered. Simple lags which say that ticket sales in one period depend on the circumstances encountered by passengers on their last previous rail journey would indicate that (for long distance journeys) the explanatory variables might be lagged several months. Whereas the simple distributed lag scheme shown above lagged all the explanatory variable effects in the same way, with simple lags there is no reason why one should not lag one variable by one period, another by two periods, and a third not at all. Different combinations of lags could be tested by putting them all into a simple equation, but care would have to be paid to multicollinearity. Probably better is to run separate models and compare $\bar{R}^2$ statistics.

3.3   Past work

Jones and Nichols (1983) could find only three published studies of the demand for Inter City rail travel in the UK, which they describe as follows:

> The first, Evans (1969), used data from one-day before-and-after on-train surveys to estimate the effects of a major electrification scheme on rail traffic. The second, Leake (1971), examined the modal split of air and rail travellers for a small sample of inter-city journeys. The third, Tyler and Hassard (1971), estimated a gravity-type model to explain variations in the volume of rail travellers between London and a set of provincial centres.

Of these, the methodology of Evans is of doubtful accuracy, given the large day to day fluctuations that exist in rail traffic and the failure to control for other influences, and has not subsequently been used in UK work in this field. The work of Leake was followed up by work at TRRL, being published as McLeod, Everest and Paulley (1980), and Jenkins, Abbie, Everest and Paulley (1981). This TRRL work started by considering rail and air traffic between London and Scotland with standard econometric methods; then switched to Box-Jenkins methods; and finally applied Box-Jenkins analysis to a large number of passenger flows throughout the country. Only the London-Scotland work has been published, but this will be sufficient for us to comment on the methods used, in the next section.

The work by Tyler and Hassard was cross-section based rather than time series based. The variables introduced, and the resulting elasticities, are shown in Table 3.1. Cross-section elasticities are usually taken to reflect the long run situation whereas time series elasticities reflect short run effects, not for example taking account of a rail price rise's delayed effect on household and job location decisions. For this reason cross section elasticities are usually larger than time series elasticities. This appears to have held for the Tyler and Hassard work, but further objections have been raised that elasticities may have been biased upwards. One problem is simultaneity induced by rail management implicitly or explicitly taking account of volume when deciding fare and service levels. For example, a busier than average service might be given extra trains to carry the load, thereby improving frequency and possibly permitting some trains to omit some stops and improve journey times. Similarly, if the busiest routes are electrified first, these routes will receive service level improvements, (and in the UK at least) a relatively lower price as the lower variable costs of the electrified service are passed on. Jones and Nichols concluded that for this reason, as Tyler and Hassard had not estimated a pair of simultaneous relationships, their elasticities would be biased upwards.

Jones and Nichols, themselves, used ordinary least squares regression on four weekly data for seventeen London based routes for various periods between the beginning of 1969 and the middle of 1977. Despite using such short observations their investigations led them to reject the use of lagged formulations. This was almost certainly a mistake since received wisdom suggests that service improvements take several months before having anything like their full effect on demand, and something similar is taken to apply to price changes. The result is that several of the Durbin-Watson statistics reported by Jones and Nichols are worryingly low, and their elasticity estimates are noticeably lower than those of other authors.

Since the Jones and Nichols paper we have published the results of a study of our own (Fowkes, Nash and Whiteing, 1985). This paper used pooled time series and cross section data for flows between ten areas, annually. Because of the use of annual data it was not necessary to include a lag structure, all adjustments in the

27

dependent variable being assumed to be very largely completed in the same year as the responsible change in the dependent variable. The difficulty, discussed above, of not being able satisfactorily to ascribe differences of levels of flows on various routes to route specific variables, was overcome by taking first differences of the data. Hence we no longer need to assume ticket data coverage is constant from route to route, but merely that it was not changing over time as between routes. Even this assumption was optimistic as it was known that rebooking changes were occurring more on some routes, and ticket machines were also tending to fail more on some routes. Nevertheless, our area data was sufficiently spatially aggregated for us to hope that these problems would not materially affect our results.

Table 3.1
The MONICA model

(elasticities with t statistics in brackets)

Population	0.77	(10.19)
Rail fare per journey	-1.19	(9.85)
Mean rail speed*	140.6	(5.30)
Mean road speed	-0.84	(1.89)
% of households without children	1.62	(3.93)
% of households retired	-1.18	(3.68)
Hotel beds per 1000 inhabitants	0.19	(2.52)
% of workers in posts, telecommunications	0.49	(2.92)
% of workers in rail transport	0.19	(2.57)
% of workers in air, sea transport	0.10	(1.89)

$R^2 = 0.91$ with 53 degrees of freedom

*   This variable was entered in a non constant elasticity form. The result corresponds to an elasticity of 1.4 at 100 k.m.p.h.

Source: Tyler and Hassard (1973)

Year on year percentage changes in traffic were regressed on a variety of explanatory variables. This procedure combines some of the features of control flow analysis with regression analysis. Important variables are introduced explicitly, but any systematic unexplained growth in traffic will also be disallowed when estimating the effect of service variations.

Over the period in question (1972-81), traffic in total fluctuated, ending up some six per cent down. But this masked some major differences by type of route. The biggest loss of traffic was on shorter non-London based routes, being the only type of route on which fares were not reduced in real terms. Broadly, three types of explanatory variable were introduced to explain these trends. Firstly, real fares were a highly significant factor, with an average elasticity of -0.86. Secondly, variables representing the exogenous state of the economy were introduced, with employment, earnings and car ownership all highly significant. Increases in employment tended to raise rail travel, whilst earnings and car ownership had the reverse effect. Finally, variables representing the quality of service of rail and of principal competitors were added. It appeared that the introduction of improved shuttle air services from London to Manchester and Scotland had deprived rail of some eight per cent of traffic on these routes, whilst deregulation of express coach services had on average reduced rail demand by thirteen per cent. The principal improvements to rail services were brought about by introduction of the 200 km.p.h. High Speed diesel Train and by electrification. The mean effect of the High Speed Train on traffic was found to be of the order of fifteen per cent growth in traffic over the course of two years; that of the extension of the West Coast Main Line electrification to Glasgow was slightly higher. The results for London based routes are summarised in Table 3.2.

More recently, further econometric work using ordinary least squares on four weekly data has been carried out for British Rail by A.D. Owen and G.D.A. Phillips. They reworked the seventeen Jones and Nichols routes using a lagged endogenous variable to give a suitable lag structure, and then proceeded to investigate further routes of interest to British Rail (Owen and Phillips, 1987).

Table 3.2
Pooled time series regressions for all London-based routes

(elasticities with t statistics in brackets)

Fares	-0.86	(14.94)
Employment	2.15	(5.47)
Car ownership	-1.30	(4.22)
High speed train (year 1)	11%	(4.04)
High speed train (year 2)	4%	(2.37)
Time trend	2% p.a.	(1.37)

$R^2 = 0.8255$

Source: Fowkes, Nash and Whiteing (1985)

A reasonable degree of consistency was found in fares and GDP elasticities (the latter being the economic activity variable used). The mean fares elasticity was found to be -1, and that for GDP 1.4. The wide range of results obtained for the effects of the High Speed Train is illustrated in Table 3.3. The biggest effects were found at Bath and Swindon which as well as enjoying the greatest improvement in service in terms of speed and frequency, are the closest stations in the sample to London.

Table 3.3
Per cent increase in traffic due to High Speed Train on selected routes to/from London time series regression results

	First class	Standard class	Total
Bath	84	43	54
Swindon	112	30	42
Cardiff	57	27	34
Bristol	55	26	28
York	22	17	23
Leeds	28	15	19
Plymouth	0	0	0
Median of 12 flows	32	16	23

Source: Owen and Phillips (1987)

The increase in traffic may therefore include some commuting from areas which were previously thought to be outside the London commuter belt. Increases on the East Coast route to York and Leeds are rather lower, whilst to Plymouth (a route dominated by leisure traffic, and over which the full speed potential could only be used for a short distance) no significant effect could be found. It is interesting to note the degree to which increases were greater in first class traffic than in standard; this of course implies that the total increase in revenue will be considerably greater than the increase in traffic.

The overall impression of the High Speed Train created by the studies was of a journey time elasticity of the order of -0.8. That is, a one per cent rise in speed was accompanied by a 0.8 per cent rise in traffic. However, there was some sign (not borne out by the Plymouth example above) that traffic increased by a certain amount when the high speed train was introduced regardless of the extent of the time saving produced; conversely the increase in traffic was found to be less in the small number of cases where a major speed improvement had been introduced without new rolling stock. This led to an alternative hypothesis that something like half of the increased traffic was due to the improved comfort and 'image' of the new rolling stock, with a true journey time elasticity of around -0.4 (as earlier argued by Shilton, 1982). Subsequent 'Stated Preference' work has tended to confirm the elasticity of -0.8.

3.4   The Box-Jenkins approach

Box-Jenkins techniques are essentially short term forecasting techniques, smoothing the dependent variable with an appropriately chosen moving average, and making appropriate (partial lag) adjustments to allow for autocorrelation. Explanatory (independent) variables can be introduced into the formulation, so that ordinary least squares regression models can be viewed as a subset of Box-Jenkins models. However, using the Box-Jenkins methods needs considerable skill and expertise, and there is little chance that a simple reality would be modelled as such. Although multiple regression has many well known limitations, it is well understood and produces results which can be competently appraised by very many people. Box-Jenkins methods, on the other hand, are much more complex and subjective.

There has been a large scale application of Box-Jenkins techniques to a large number of UK point to point rail flows, but the results of this work remain commercial in confidence. The only part of this work that has been published, to our knowledge, deals with London to Scotland traffic. The first of the two papers, McLeod, Everest and Paulley (1980) dealt with London-Glasgow traffic (both for rail and air). The results published were overtaken by those in the next paper, Jenkins, Abbie, Everest and Paulley (1981). This dealt with both Edinburgh and Glasgow to London data. The rail price elasticities derived were considerably different to those in the later work, so it would be misleading to quote them here. The rail journey time elasticities were around -1.3, but barely significant. While many will feel that further application of Box-Jenkins techniques is the obvious way forward, experience to date has not been too encouraging, even in expert hands. Our view is that the classical econometric approach, discussed earlier, still represents the best technique.

3.5   Conclusion

We have seen, then, that aggregate econometric studies using ticket sales data are capable of producing a great deal of valuable information about rail demand.   Robust estimates of price elasticities of demand have been achieved, together with some understanding both of the effects of rail service quality and of external factors such as the state of the economy.

However, there are many questions this approach has left unanswered. In the first place, no very good evidence on the effect of small changes in service quality (e.g. frequency, comfort or the need to change trains) has been produced by this approach. The reason is that on most InterCity routes, such changes have been modest and their effect has been lost in the noise produced by the various data problems discussed earlier.

Secondly, these studies have not been able to disaggregate results on elasticities, for instance, by the type of person travelling or the purpose of their journey. Yet for many marketing purposes (e.g. designing new fares structures or bargain offers) such information is very important.

For both these reasons, extensive use has also been made of disaggregate methods, particularly using Stated Preference data. It is to these methods that we turn in the next chapter.

4 Disaggregate methods

TONY FOWKES AND MARK WARDMAN

4.1 Introduction

This chapter discusses disaggregate methods of analysing travel behaviour. The aim is to provide a general introduction to the disaggregate approach by examining the basic methodology, alternative sources of data, and its advantages and limitations.

The feature which distinguishes the disaggregate modelling approach is that it focusses on the individual decision maker. The dependent variable reflects an individual's preferences amongst travel alternatives, such as destinations, modes or routes, and variations in these choices across individuals are explained by reference to their different personal and travel characteristics. Thus they contrast with the aggregate methods discussed in the previous chapter which are based on measures of collective behaviour such as market shares and travel flows.

Disaggregate methods are of comparatively recent origin. Much of the pioneering work was undertaken in the transport field in the 1970's, and although many contributed to the work, it is generally held that McFadden made the single greatest contribution (eg. McFadden, 1974; 1981).

The advantages of disaggregate methods largely stem from their avoidance of aggregating and averaging. Disaggregate models are claimed to provide a firmer behavioural basis, in the sense that the models are based on an explicit theory of consumer behaviour and aim to explain causality rather than capture correlations. They avoid the problems arising from using zonally averaged travel data. For example, the process of averaging the independent variables to represent the different travel characteristics of travellers from a particular zone can lead to relatively little 'between group' variation, despite quite high 'within group' variation, such that their effects cannot be reliably estimated. Good examples are walking and waiting times for public transport, which often vary little when taken as zonal averages but which can be expected to vary greatly across individuals. Disaggregate models can exploit this rich source of information. Moreover, the process of averaging the independent variables can lead to seriously biased parameter estimates and forecasts (McFadden and Reid, 1974). Disaggregate methods facilitate market segmentation since each individual's responses can be directly related to their socio-economic characteristics. Indeed, aggregate travel data and socio-economic indicators are not always available but the relevant disaggregate data can be collected. In addition, disaggregate methods can use data collected from hypothetical questioning methods in addition to behaviour observed in the market place, such data being known in the UK as Stated Preference data.

Richards (1980) commented that "Disaggregate models have been presented if not as a Utopia certainly as a panacea". Whilst disaggregate methods certainly have a number of attractions in many instances, some of the claimed advantages can turn out to be rather illusory. In well defined applications, quite small samples could provide good modelling estimates for the parameters of interest. However, in other applications, even 1,000 observations might prove insufficient to obtain reliable estimates. This has often been the case with studies of the value of travel time, where 95 per cent confidence intervals typically ± 100 per cent of the central estimate have not been uncommon (MVA, ITS, TSU, 1987), for reasons which will be discussed below. Nonetheless, disaggregate methods do have a number of attractions in many instances, particularly their ability to support Stated Preference analysis.

4.2   Theoretical background

The conventional economic theory of consumer behaviour posits that each individual aims to maximise utility within their overall time and income constraints and that they will choose that travel alternative from the k (modes, routes, destinations, etc.) on offer which yields highest indirect utility (MVA et al., 1987). However, the analyst cannot possibly recognise and measure all the factors which influence each individual's utility and choice, whilst some attributes are excluded from consideration as having only a minor influence upon choice. An error term (ε_k) is therefore introduced to represent the net effect of omitted variables. An alternative's (random) utility (U_k) is therefore assumed to consist of a deterministic component (V_k) which can be estimated, and which is often termed representative utility, and the unobservable error term:

$$U_k = V_k + \varepsilon_k \qquad (4.1)$$

If only time (T) and cost (C) influence choice, a simple linear-additive representative utility function for alternative k would take the form:

$$V_k = \alpha_{tk}T_k + \alpha_{ck}C_k \qquad (4.2)$$

where the subscript k denotes that the utility weights as well as time and cost can vary across alternatives; for example, if the time coefficient differs between modes according to their comfort. Note that the utility weights will be negative since T and C are not 'goods' but 'bads'.

We can observe C_k and T_k and therefore obtain some estimate of V_k. Since ε_k is unobservable, the analysis of travel behaviour must proceed on the basis of V_k alone. However, we cannot be certain that, say, option 1 will be preferred if V_1 is highest since the error term may influence the outcome. We would, however, expect that the likelihood of choosing option 1 increases as V_1 increases. The probability that an individual chooses option 1 from the k alternatives available can be represented as:

$$P_1 = \text{Prob} \left[(V_1 + \varepsilon_1) > (V_k + \varepsilon_k) \right] \qquad \text{for all k, k} \neq 1 \qquad (4.3)$$

By assuming some probability distribution for the ε_k, the probability of individuals choosing option 1 can be specified solely as a function of the estimable component of utility (V_k). Assuming that the errors associated with each option have a type I extreme value (Weibull) distribution (independent and identical) yields the commonly used logit model (McFadden, 1974):

$$P_1 = \exp(\Omega V_1)/\Sigma_k \exp(\Omega V_k) \qquad (4.4)$$

As a result of the widespread availability of estimation packages and its relative simplicity, this is the most widely used model for the analysis of discrete choice data. Where choices are made amongst just two alternatives, the logit model simplifies to:

$$P_1 = 1/\{1 + \exp[\Omega(V_2 - V_1)]\} \tag{4.5}$$

The disaggregate logit model's coefficients are estimated by maximum likelihood to provide the best explanation of individuals' discrete choices. The parameter Ω is a scaling factor and we introduce it here since it is important in a subsequent discussion in section 4.7 concerning the use of Stated Preference models for forecasting. Ω is related to the standard deviation of the errors association with each alternative $(\sigma_{\varepsilon k})$:

$$\Omega = \pi/(6\sigma_{\varepsilon k}) \tag{4.6}$$

Ω applies to all the coefficients equally and hence it does not affect their relative magnitudes. However, it does influence the absolute coefficient estimates. The purpose of Ω is essentially to scale the coefficients to allow for the effect of the unobserved influences (ε_k) on choice.

The main drawback of the logit model is what is termed its Independence of Irrelevant Alternatives (IIA) property. This stems from its restrictive assumption that the error terms are independent. To illustrate this problem, suppose that there are only two modes, namely car and bus. Their relative logit choice probabilities are:

$$P_c/P_b = \exp[\Omega(V_c - V_b)] \tag{4.7}$$

This ratio is unaffected by the expansion of the choice set. For example, if train is introduced and captures ten per cent of the market, both car and bus will be predicted to lose ten per cent of their shares. The IIA property is clearly undesirable if we expect train to attract disproportionately more from bus than from car so that P_c/P_b will increase.

Different assumptions regarding the distribution of the ε_k will yield different models. Assuming the errors to have a multivariate Normal distribution yields the multinominal probit model (Ben-Akiva and Lerman, 1985). This does not suffer from the IIA problem, although it is a much more complex model, reflected in its far less widespread use, and indeed it becomes intractable for more than a few alternatives.

The problems arising from the multinominal logit model's IIA property are avoided by the hierarchical or nested logit model. This model, which can be regarded as state of the art practice, allows for differential substitutability between modes by specifying a series of sub-choices or nests within a hierarchical structure. In the case of the choice between train, car and bus, this might involve modelling the choice between car and public transport consequent upon modelling the choice between train and bus. The modelling of the choice between train and bus in the lower nest provides a 'composite cost' term which represents the attractiveness of public transport in relation to car in the upper nest. The structure can be extended, for example, to examine the choice of access mode to train or the choice between different train departures. Although this model is less straightforward than the multinominal logit model, it is a far more practical solution than the probit model (see Preston, 1987, and chapter 8 of this book for a discussion of the hierarchical logit model and its application to forecasting rail demand).

There are two purposes for which disaggregate models are estimated. The coefficient estimates can be used for inter-attribute valuation, such as value of time estimation. These values can be used directly to assess the welfare implications of specific actions, as in cost-benefit analysis, or can be used indirectly for forecasting. The coefficient estimates can also be used directly for forecasting market share.

Valuation

Given estimates of the utility weights and hence the relative importance of the attributes, it is a simple process to obtain estimates of relative values such as the money value of time. The latter is the ratio of the marginal utilities of time and money. Estimates of scale transformations of these marginal utilities are derived by differentiating the utility function with respect to time and money. In a linear-additive utility function, as in equation 4.2, an estimate of the value of travel time for alternative k is simply derived as the ratio of its time and cost coefficients $(\alpha_{tk}/\alpha_{ck})$.

Forecasting

The conventional means of forecasting with disaggregate models is to use what is termed the *probabilistic* method. Using the logit model of equation 4.4, each individual's probability of choosing, say, alternative 1 (P_1) is calculated on the basis of the estimated parameters and their relevant travel and personal circumstances. Aggregate market shares are then derived as the grossed up sum of these individual choice probabilities. This avoids potential biases which are introduced if aggregate market share forecasts are derived in a single calculation using variables which are averaged across all individuals. This problem arises because the relationship between P_k and V_k is non-linear. For a further discussion of aggregation issues, the interested reader is referred to Ben-Akiva and Lerman (1985, Ch.6).

In contrast, the *deterministic* forecasting method, which has been widely used in marketing research, assigns an individual to that option with highest deterministic utility (V_k), and hence highest probability, on an all-or-nothing basis, and aggregate market shares are obtained as the grossed up sum of the individual 0-1 predicted choices. The drawback of this approach is that, unlike the probabilistic method, it does not account for the effect of the unobservable influences on choices since it is based solely on the observable utility component.

4.3   Comparison of disaggregate methods

Within the disaggregate modelling framework we shall distinguish between three methods according to the nature of the input data used. These are termed Revealed Preference (RP), Stated Preference (SP) and Transfer Price (TP), and we will discuss issues concerning each of these in turn.

Revealed Preference methods

RP models are based on individuals' reported or observed behaviour along with the travel attributes and personal circumstances which give rise to that behaviour. It is natural to approach the consideration of the various disaggregate methods with a strong prejudice in favour of working with data on actual decisions that have taken place. A person who was faced with more than one course of action and actually took one particular course of action and rejected the others reveals something about the relative importance attached to the variables which influence the choice.

However, suppose that the only factors taken into account are time and cost. By observing that a person chooses a course of action in preference to the next best alternative, all that one can in fact deduce is which side of a particular threshold his value of time

38

lies. It is only by putting together a list of decisions of a particular kind being made by a similar set of people that one is able to narrow down to a single value of time which is most consistent with the evidence. Usually, we have only one RP observation per individual. We need to interview/observe a number of individuals all facing a similar choice, such as the choice of mode for the journey to work. More than this we need data which is informative, that is, individuals in the sample should, taken together, have faced a range of 'boundary values' for their choices.

Suppose that coach and train are the only two modes available and that time and cost are the only attributes influencing choice. The journey times and costs will vary across individuals. Hence the choice facing each individual will contain an implicit 'boundary value of time' (BVOT), which, in the absence of any mode specific preferences, will be:

$$BVOT = (C_t - C_c)/(T_c - T_t) \qquad (4.8)$$

Subject to some random components which we allow for in behaviour, to cover those aspects not explicitly modelled, an individual will choose the faster mode if his value of time is greater than BVOT. If, for example:

$C_t = £2.30$ $C_c = £2.00$
$T_t = 50$ mins $T_c = 60$ mins

the boundary value of time would be:

$BVOT = 30/10 = 3$ pence per minute

Individuals with values of time greater than three pence per minute will choose train.

We cannot always assume that each individual will be facing a trade-off. In the above example, for instance, although train is generally a faster mode than coach, it may be that the coach stop is much more convenient for some individuals than is the rail station. If T_c was, say, five minutes less than T_t, BVOT would be negative (−6p/min). Negative boundary values indicate that one alternative dominates the other in the attributes being considered; here coach is both quicker and faster. Learning that an individual's value of time is greater than −6p/min is unlikely to be much help to us!

We therefore seek situations where choices are not dominated. This may rule out car versus train RP mode choice studies, in

39

situations where respondents regard the car as quicker and cheaper. If we manage to avoid dominated choices, we still require that the choices exhibit a good range of (positive) boundary values. This can be a problem where, to continue our example above, cost and time differences between alternatives are positively correlated. This can easily occur in practice as, for each mode, longer journeys are more costly and take more time. If fares were charged at a simple rate per mile and speeds were constant for all journey lengths for a given mode, we would have:

$$C_t = \text{MILES * TRAIN FARE PER MILE}$$
$$C_c = \text{MILES * COACH FARE PER MILE}$$
$$T_t = \text{MILES/TRAIN SPEED}$$
$$T_c = \text{MILES/COACH SPEED}$$

$$\text{BVOT} = \frac{\text{MILES * (train fare per mile} - \text{coach fare per mile)}}{\text{MILES * [(1/coach speed)} - \text{(1/train speed)]}} \quad (4.9)$$

The MILES term cancels and all the other terms are assumed constant so there is just one BVOT for all journey lengths! Our data will tell us merely what percentage of our respondents' values of time lie on each side of this BVOT.

A particularly successful mode choice RP study was carried out in North Kent in 1983 as part of the Department of Transport Value of Time Study (Fowkes, 1986). Rail and coach commuters into Central London were interviewed. By design and some good fortune, the time and cost differences came out negatively correlated, largely due to the range of access distances to the suburban rail stations and to the coach stops. Consequently, there was a great variation in the degree to which the door to door rail time was faster by rail than by coach. Hence there was a good range of BVOT's in the data. The possible correlation effect referred to above was avoided by sampling commuters making journeys all of similar distances, such that the cost difference between rail and coach was similar for all respondents. Nevertheless, the 95 per cent confidence interval on the value of in-vehicle time estimate was $\pm$ 33 per cent, and somewhat more for the values of walking and waiting time, indicating that even a good RP experiment with about 1,000 responses still yields rather imprecise estimates. Naturally, values of time disaggregated by sex or by income were even more imprecisely estimated.

Transfer Price methods

The first alternative to RP data that we shall consider makes use of what has been termed Transfer Price (TP) data. Lee and Dalvi (1969) first proposed the use of TP data in the context of Value of Time estimation. A TP question would follow something along the lines of:

> By how much would the cost of your chosen alternative have to rise in order for you to switch to your next best alternative?

In essence, the answer can be taken as an estimate of the utility difference between the chosen and rejected alternatives expressed in this case in money units. If only time and cost influence the choice between train and coach, and train is currently preferred to coach, then the TP response allows the following equality to be specified:

$$C_t + (VOT^*T_t) + TP = C_c + (VOT^*T_c) \qquad (4.10)$$

Unlike equation (4.8), which indicates only a boundary value of time, equation (4.10) can be solved for VOT, and therein lies the advantage of the TP method in that it provides much more information per individual response.

In the more general case where choice is influenced by variables other than time and cost, the TP response can then be regressed on the reported attributes to arrive at attribute coefficients. For example, if frequency (F) also influences choice and there is a mode specific constant denoting a preference for one mode over the other *ceteris paribus*, the TP model could take the form of:

$$TP = \alpha_0 + \alpha_1 (C_c - C_t) + \alpha_2 (T_c - T_t) + \alpha_3 (F_c - F_t) \qquad (4.11)$$

If the TP responses are in the same units as cost, α_1 should equal one whereupon α_2 and α_3 can be directly taken as the values of time and frequency respectively.

Alternative formulations of the TP question can be based on other continuous variables, such as in-vehicle, walk and wait time (in which case it is sometimes referred to as a Transfer Time), whilst it is possible to enquire as to the minimum necessary reduction in some attribute of an alternative option which would cause a change in behaviour.

The TP approach has generally been used for inter-attribute

valuation (Lee and Dalvi, 1969; 1971; Hensher, 1976; Broom et al, 1983; Gunn, 1984) but it potentially contains much relevant information for forecasting purposes. Since the TP response indicates that point at which a change of behaviour occurs, it is possible to obtain elasticity measures by calculating the proportion of travellers who would change behaviour after a proportionate change in price, all other things equal. However, the results of TP studies have generally been unconvincing and it would be fair to say that TP methods are regarded with not a little scepticism in many quarters. Sample sizes are often greatly reduced (in a non-random way) by some individuals being unable or unwilling to provide a monetary TP. Those responses that are in monetary units are not scaled consistently with actual monetary expenditures.

4.4   Overview of Stated Preference techniques

Unlike TP methods, SP methods have been quite favourably received within the transport field, and have become a widely used analytical tool. Stated Preference is used as a generic term to encompass a number of variations upon a basic theme of offering individuals a series of hypothetical travel scenarios amongst which they express a preference. The responses provide information on the relative importance of the attributes contained in the experiment.

The distinction made here between various forms of Stated Preference technique follows that used by Bates (1988) and Louviere (1988) and is based on whether the responses take the form of choices, rankings or ratings.

Choice

Respondents can be asked to make choices between (usually two) travel alternatives along the lines of actual decision making. Each alternative is described in terms of the variables which may influence choice. Practical applications rarely contain more than five attributes per alternative (with all else held constant) and the number of choices presented to each individual usually lies between nine and sixteen. However, there is little empirical evidence regarding the optimal number of choices or attributes to offer. Whilst presenting more choices yields more information, it also increases the chances of respondent fatigue, boredom and annoyance, with implications for the quality of the responses and the response rate. The task will also become more difficult as the number of attributes increases. Table 4.1 provides an example of a choice SP experiment which was used in a study of the demand for a new rail service between Leicester and Burton on Trent and which is reported in Chapter 8.

Table 4.1
Example of choice SP experiment

	In-veh. time	Out-of veh. time	Fare	Frequency	Choice
Train	15mins	5mins	55p	Every 2hrs	[ ]
Bus	25mins	10mins	55p	as now	[ ]

The theoretical and statistical framework provided by the disaggregate random utility models discussed above has obvious attractions for the analysis of Stated Preference responses if they are in the form of discrete choices. The most commonly used model to analyse Stated Preference choice data is disaggregate logit.

Ranking

An individual can be presented with n alternatives to be ranked in order of preference. In practice, the number of alternatives to be ranked often lies between eight and twelve, although it can be as few as four or five where multiple ranking exercises are presented. However, the task will become more difficult as the number of alternatives to be ranked increases and the quality of the data collected can be expected to fall. Each alternative can contain the full profile of relevant attributes or a sub-set of them. Table 4.2 provides an example of a ranking experiment which was used in the study of business travellers reported in Chapter 5.

Table 4.2
Example of ranking SP experiment

	COST £	Leave home	Arrive home	Rank
AIR	80	07.00	18.30	- - - -
RAIL 1ST	75	06.30	20.00	- - - -
RAIL 2ND	50	06.30	20.00	- - - -
CAR	40	05.30	20.30	- - - -

The usual means of analysing ranked SP data is to use the ordered or exploded logit model (Chapman and Staelin, 1982). This model treats the ranking of n alternatives as a series of choices across n−1 choice sets and multinominal logit is simultaneously applied to the preference for the first ranked option over the other n−1 options, the preference for the second ranked over the remaining n−2 options and so on until the ranking exhausts the series of implied choices. Alternatively the ranking can be exploded to pairwise choices.

Rating

This approach involves a response on a numeric or semantic scale. A numeric scale elicits a rating of each alternative on a scale of say 1−100 and the response is taken to indicate the strength and not just the order of preference. A semantic scale yields responses which are somewhere between the continuous data of a numeric rating and the ordinal data of discrete choices. Five point scales are the most common. Table 4.3 presents an example of a semantic rating SP experiment which was used in the analysis of long distance rail travellers' valuations of changes in time, frequency and reliability, and which is discussed in Chapter 7.

Table 4.3
Example of semantic rating scale SP experiment

	A	B
FARE	One way: £5.50 Return: £11	One way: £4.50 Return: £9
SCHEDULED TIME MAXIMUM DELAY	1 hour 30 mins Up to 10 mins late	1 hour 50 mins Up to 0 mins late
TIMETABLE	Trains leave EVERY HOUR	Trains leave EVERY 4 HOURS
Manchester dep: Birmingham arr:	8:30 9:30 10:30 11:30 10:00 11:00 12:00 1:00	8:00 12:00 9:50 1:50

Definitely prefer A   [   ]
Probably prefer A   [   ]
Like A and B equally   [   ]
Probably prefer B   [   ]
Definitely prefer B   [   ]

Where the preferences between two alternatives are expressed on a semantic scale, the most straightforward way to model them is to assign values to the responses to represent the utility difference between the two alternatives and apply multiple regression (Kocur et al., 1982a; Louviere and Kocur, 1983). What is effectively the same approach results from assigning values to the responses to represent the probability of using an option (P_1) in, say, a logit model (Bates and Roberts, 1983). Equation (4.5) would be transformed to be suitable for estimation by multiple linear regression, whereupon the dependent variable would take the form $Ln[P_1/(1-P_1)]$. Commonly used probabilities of using alternative 1 for the responses of 'definitely prefer alternative 1' through to 'definitely prefer alternative 2' are 0.9, 0.7, 0.5, 0.3 and 0.1. These imply a rating scale of 2.20, 0.85, 0.00, −0.85 and −2.20. Although the relative values obtained from this logit model are insensitive to the assumptions made in transforming the responses into probabilities, a major drawback is that the absolute coefficients and hence the choice probabilities are affected by the assumptions made.

Where the SP data is of the form of a continuous rating of alternatives, multiple regression can be applied to estimate the weights associated with the attributes (Hensher and Truong, 1983).

4.5   Issues in the design of Stated Preference experiments

Given a specific form of Stated Preference method which is to be used, the design stage requires decisions as to the number of scenarios, the number of variables and the number of levels that each variable can take, although these are not independent decisions. The conventional approach is to combine the levels in such a manner that the variables are uncorrelated. Table 4.4 presents such an orthogonal design.

Consider the first two columns of Table 4.4, that is, variables A and B. Both variables have three levels and all possible combinations occur to yield nine scenarios. This is termed a full factorial design. The main effects, that is the separate effects of A and B, are completely uncorrelated and are unconfounded with the interaction term. If there are r variables with X levels, s variables with Y levels and t variables with Z levels, a full factorial design will contain $X^r Y^s Z^t$ scenarios which rapidly becomes too large for practical purposes as the number of levels or the number of variables increase.

Fractional factorial designs are used when a full factorial design generates too many scenarios, and catalogues of such designs are available (Kocur et al., 1982b). These omit some of the possible combinations whilst maintaining zero main effect correlations, albeit at the expense of the number of interactions which can still be estimated and the extent to which the main effects are unconfounded with two factor interactions.

The first two columns of Table 4.4 constitute the basic framework or skeleton design expressed as 'levels of difference' between the two alternatives that constitute the scenario. It remains to assign judiciously chosen values to the levels. As the values increasingly diverge from individuals' experiences or from what appears plausible, the responses can be expected to become less reliable. Computer interactive interview techniques are of use in customising the basic framework to an individual's particular circumstances (Bradley, 1988).

The main advantages of orthogonal designs are that they ensure that the independent effects of the attributes can be disentangled. However, Fowkes and Wardman (1988) argue that orthogonality does not automatically ensure a satisfactory design. If cost and two other attributes enter the design, departing from orthogonality can allow greater emphasis on getting a valuation of one of these other two attributes in money terms, ie. reducing the standard error of estimate. In addition, we emphasised the need to ensure that the trade-offs between attributes are such that they will allow the accurate estimation of underlying relative values.

Table 4.4
An orthogonal design

	BASIC DESIGN		NUMERICAL EXAMPLE		
	Var A	Var B	Time Var A	Cost Var B	Boundary
	(Differences)		(Differences)		Values
SCENARIO 1	1	1	−10	15	1.50
SCENARIO 2	1	2	−10	25	2.50
SCENARIO 3	1	3	−10	40	4.00
SCENARIO 4	2	1	−15	15	1.00
SCENARIO 5	2	2	−15	25	1.67
SCENARIO 6	2	3	−15	40	2.67
SCENARIO 7	3	1	−20	15	0.75
SCENARIO 8	3	2	−20	25	1.25
SCENARIO 9	3	3	−20	40	2.00

Consider the columns headed by time and cost in Table 4.4, which are based on the full factorial design for variables A and B, and suppose that the design forms the basis of nine pairwise comparisons where only time and cost influence choice. The actual values attached to the levels in this example are in difference form between the two alternatives (−10, −15, −20 for time and 15, 25 and 40 for cost). The final column denotes the boundary value of time at which the individual would be indifferent between the two options.

Assigning realistic values to the levels in an orthogonal design does not automatically produce a satisfactory experimental design: it does not necessarily imply inter-attribute trade-offs let alone a satisfactory range of boundary values. The boundary values range from 0.75 to 4.00 in the above example and, although this would be fine if individuals' values were generally around 2, the design would provide little useful information if individuals' values were centred around 8 (eg. business travellers). Care must be taken to ensure that trade-offs used cover a sufficiently large range of boundary values so that the Stated Preference responses can allow the accurate estimation of the actual underlying values for any subgroup for which valuations are required. This may necessitate a movement away from an orthogonal design.

Not only should the attribute values used be realistic, but the values should be combined in a realistic manner. The need to follow a specific pattern in combining levels of variables in order to achieve orthogonality may give rise to combinations that are physically impossible or highly unrealistic, with potentially serious consequences for the quality of the data obtained. In a motorists' route choice context, for example, the correlations between distance, journey time, speed and petrol cost must be allowed for. Orthogonality can also be lost in certain circumstances, for example, when variables from outside the experiment are entered into the Stated Preference model or are used to modify the variables in the design before estimation. When different orthogonal designs are used for different sub-sets of the population, perhaps in order to customise the design to individuals' particular circumstances, the variables in a model based on more than one design are not necessarily uncorrelated.

4.6 Testing the adequacy of the experimental design

It is not generally a straightforward matter to design satisfactory Stated Preference experiments, and we are aware of orthogonal SP designs which have been used which contain serious deficiencies because they neglected to examine the implied boundary values.

Although the boundary values are immediately apparent in the two variable example of Table 4.4, this will not be so when there are more than two variables in the design and the implied boundary value for one variable depends on the relative value of other variables (see Fowkes, 1991). The issue therefore becomes more complex as the number of variables increases. It is recommended that simulation tests using synthetic data are conducted to ensure that the design is capable of recovering accurate estimates of a series of relative values which are chosen in order to reflect the range of possibilities that could realistically arise, not just for the sample as a whole but any subgroups for which values are required, eg. business travellers. Designs which are found to be inadequate are rejected or modified. If departures are made from an orthogonal design, such simulation tests would also indicate whether the non-zero correlations between attributes cause serious confounding effects.

Table 4.5

Experimental design for estimating overcrowding
and departure time variations

| | -----------OPTION A----------- | | | -----------OPTION B----------- | | |
	FARE	SEAT	DEPTIME	FARE	SEAT	DEPTIME
1	A	FULL	A	+50p	PLENTY	A
2	−£1	FULL	A	A	PLENTY	A
3	A	FULL	A	+£2	PLENTY	A
4	−50p	STAND30	A	A	PLENTY	A
5	A	STAND30	A	+£1	PLENTY	A
6	−£2	STAND30	A	A	PLENTY	A
7	A	STAND30	A	+£5	PLENTY	A
8	A	STAND60	A	+£2	FULL	A
9	A	STAND60	A	+£5	FULL	A
10	A	STAND60	A	+£10	FULL	A
11	A	STAND60	1HR	+£5	PLENTY	A
12	A	STAND60	1HR	+£10	PLENTY	A
13	A	STAND60	1HR	+£20	PLENTY	A
14	A	FULL	2HR	+£1	FULL	A
15	A	FULL	2HR	+£5	FULL	A
16	A	FULL	2HR	+£40	FULL	A

NOTE: DEPTIME and FARE are specified as changes to the actual journey. 'A' denotes that the variable is at the same level as for the actual journey made. PLENTY implies that the passenger gets a good choice of seat, FULL implies that the passenger gets a seat but the train is full with others standing, and STAND30/STAND60 imply that the passenger has to stand for the stated number of minutes.

Table 4.5 presents the experimental design which was used in the study of overcrowding and departure time variations for

InterCity travellers which is discussed in Chapter 5.

Crowding had four levels representing seated in a train with PLENTY of seats, seated but in a FULL train, standing for 30 minutes and standing for 60 minutes. Choices 1, 2, and 3 offer the choice between a FULL train and PLENTY of seats for additional payments of 50p, £1, £2 respectively. Hence the 'boundary values' for FULL against PLENTY for these three choices are 50p, £1 and £2 respectively. Provided that the true value lies in that sort of range we should be able to obtain an efficient estimate of it.

Simulation tests were conducted on this design. This involved generating 1,600 discrete choices (i.e. the responses of 100 individuals) on the basis of the experimental design values, specified utility weights and a random error term. These choices were modelled to establish whether the specified values could be recovered. The results of the simulation tests which were undertaken are presented in Table 4.6. Note that the estimates manage to track the assumed values over large ranges.

Table 4.6
Tests of the experimental design

DEPTIME	ASSUMED FULL	STAND30	STAND60	DEPTIME	ESTIMATED FULL	STAND30	STAND60
1.00	50	100	150	1.07	44	112	180
1.00	150	300	500	0.91	152	303	511
1.00	250	750	1500	0.98	236	695	1491
1.50	100	250	500	1.52	102	264	505
2.00	75	150	400	1.84	67	143	405
2.50	100	300	500	2.58	105	289	523
3.00	50	200	300	2.71	57	234	342
3.00	200	400	600	2.87	211	384	619
3.50	100	250	500	3.46	103	254	504
4.00	100	400	750	4.00	86	412	759
5.00	50	150	250	5.19	45	152	247
5.00	300	500	1000	4.69	283	521	991
8.00	150	300	750	7.44	200	291	813
10.00	50	100	200	10.53	47	96	202
15.00	150	350	1000	15.54	168	357	988
20.00	100	250	500	18.96	133	223	512
25.00	500	1000	2500	27.10	386	974	2309

Note: The value of DEPTIME is given in pence per minute. The values of the other variables are specified in pence.

In summary, the key elements of our recommendations as to how satisfactory Stated Preference designs may be achieved centred on studying boundary values and testing the design with simulated data. When there is not the time available in some circumstances for a prolonged examination of boundary values and 'fine tuning' to achieve, at times marginal, improvements to the design, the testing stage assumes greater importance in order to avoid the application of an inadequate design. In an ideal world the process is iterative, but it should be noted that such careful design work can take several weeks, followed by a field pilot and further refinement of the design.

4.7   Revealed Preference, Stated Preference and Transfer Price methods compared

The specific advantages and shortcomings of the RP, SP and TP methods will depend on the precise technique which is used and the circumstances in which it is to be used. Nonetheless, the relative merits of the three methods can be discussed in a general sense.

Revealed Preference methods

The advantage of the RP approach is that, in principle at least, actual behaviour in the market place provides the best information of the relative importance individuals place upon those factors which are influencing that behaviour. However, there are often deficiencies in the quality of this data which can lead to problems estimating the underlying influences on actual behaviour or limit the scope of the analysis.

The main limitation of the RP approach is clearly when no market exists in which individuals can reveal their preferences. An existing choice context can be deficient because there are limited trade-offs across attributes and unsatisfactory boundary values, whilst multicollinearity or insufficient variation in variables of interest may also pose problems. Even large sample sizes, as discussed above, may not produce sufficiently precise parameter estimates. RP models may also suffer from measurement error in the independent variables which can lead to inaccurate parameter estimates and forecasts (Ortuzar and Ivelic, 1987). Such measurement error may stem from: the use of engineering data which at best only approximates the perceived values upon which individuals base their decisions; the use of average attribute values; rounding error in the reported values; and justification bias, that is where the chosen option is reported to be artificially attractive as part of a process of justifying the actual choice made.

50

The deficiencies of RP methods provided a stimulus to the development of alternative data sources such as SP. Stated Preference methods are the most feasible means of approximating laboratory conditions on a large scale and their advantages stem from their ability to control the choice context and the precise details of the scenarios to be considered. This means that SP methods can avoid many of the deficiencies which can plague RP methods.

Stated Preference models overcome the most serious problem facing RP methods which arises when the required choice context does not exist, since the required choice, involving say a new mode or destination, can be created. SP experiments can control the degree of correlation and variation and thereby avoid problems of multicollinearity and insufficient variation. Furthermore, measurement error in the independent variables is avoided and variables can be examined outside the range of current or past experiences. Indeed, as was seen in the discussion of design, SP experiments can ensure that the appropriate inter-attribute trade-offs are introduced. Stated Preference experiments involve individuals in repeat evaluations of travel scenarios whereas RP models typically contain only a single observation per person. The greater amount of data, combined with SP data being 'richer' in the sense that it contains the trade-offs across attributes which are necessary for the successful calibration of choice models but which are not always widespread in practice, holds out the opportunity of obtaining more precise estimates or of reducing data collection costs in relation to RP methods.

Stated Preference data is well suited to examining alternative functional forms of the utility expression since the travel attributes generally enter at only a limited number of levels. This can be conducted by analysis of variance or piecewise estimation. If a variable enters at j levels, j-1 dummy variables are specified and the estimated coefficients represent the utility effect of moving away from the base (j'th) level of that variable. The resulting part-worth function indicates a particular functional form for the utility expression and may be of use in its own right. Another opportunity open to SP models, but which is not generally feasible with RP models, is that of being able to calibrate separate models for each individual if sufficient data per person is collected. Such models automatically allow for inter-personal taste variations. They therefore avoid potential biases at the calibration stage and allow a more precise examination of any particular individual's response to some change in travel circumstances. Studies by Beggs, Cardell and Hausman (1981), Moore (1980) and Wittink and Montgomery (1979) suggest that improved predictive performance is achieved by using individual-specific coefficients rather than a single set of coefficients for all individuals. However, this requires more data to be collected from each individual than is required for conventional modelling and so could adversely affect the quality and indeed the quantity (in terms of a lower response rate) of data. Our experience is that, in such cases, use of computerised Adaptive Stated Preference algorithms to optimise the information content of the hypothetical chances presented can sufficiently overcome respondent failure and resistance to enable individual models to be calibrated, albeit inexactly and at the cost of having individual interviews (Fowkes and Tweddle, 1988).

Whilst these advantages show that SP methods have much potential for improving our understanding of travel behaviour, there are also problems with the SP approach. The main criticism levelled at SP methods is that individuals' stated and actual preferences do not coincide because they are not committed to behave in accordance with their stated preferences; so-called non-commitment bias.

The most serious form of error is that which results from the deliberate biassing of responses since it may cause the coefficient estimates to be biased in relation to each other. Such bias in responses could stem from a desire to justify a choice actually made. Unconstrained response bias arises from a failure to incorporate all relevant constraints on behaviour when evaluating the hypothetical scenarios. In some contexts, the SP responses may be amended to accord with what is regarded to be socially acceptable. Such social-norm bias may well influence stated preferences with regard to, for example, drinking and driving.

What has been termed strategic or policy response bias is the deliberate biassing of responses in order to increase (reduce) the chances or magnitude of some favourable (adverse) change. Empirical evidence suggests that strategic bias is strongly present in crude behavioural intention data (Chatterjee, Wegmann and McAdams, 1983; Couture and Dooley, 1981). However, the invitation to strategic bias is generally considered to be less for Stated Preference experiments because they avoid placing the emphasis on changes in a single variable and it is less clear how to bias responses in order to influence policy. Furthermore, blatant attempts at deliberate biassing will (with a suitable design) give rise to otherwise rare response patterns, whence the models can be recalibrated without these particular patterns. We have a simple technique (called 'bin analysis') which, if included in the design, helps to spot such outliers (Fowkes, 1991).

Error of a more random nature, in the sense that it is less likely to affect the relative coefficient estimates, includes that arising from misunderstanding, uncertainty as to which option is preferred, not taking the exercise seriously, boredom and respondent fatigue. The amount of error in SP responses is likely to increase as the number of alternatives or attributes to be evaluated increases, or as the exercise increasingly departs from individuals' actual experiences.

No proponent of SP methods would contend that SP responses are error free. However, they can point to empirical evidence which implies a high degree of correspondence between revealed and stated preferences across individuals (Benjamin and Sen, 1982; Green and Srinivasen, 1978; Levin et al., 1983; Louviere, 1988; Timmermans, 1984; Wardman, 1988).

However, it is important to avoid over-generalisation since the extent to which SP responses accurately reflect actual preferences may depend on the precise situation being investigated and the specific form of Stated Preference technique used. Care should be taken that the SP experiment is realistic, well designed and executed, is appropriate for the purposes of the study and is not too difficult. The choice Stated Preference method has the attractions of being relatively simple for respondents and requiring responses which take the same form as the actual travel decisions made in practice. Rankings generally yield more information but they are more difficult, particularly when there are more than a few attributes. It is yet more difficult to state the strength of preference, as with a continuous rating. The empirical evidence with respect to which technique is the best in terms of the quality of data obtained is not conclusive. Some studies suggest that the different methods produce broadly similar results (Bovy and Bradley, 1985; Leigh, McKay and Summers, 1984) yet others have found somewhat large discrepancies (Bates and Roberts, 1983; MVA, ITS, TSU, 1983).

The scale factor problem

Even if the error in SP models is essentially random, there is a further problem when using them to forecast demand. The coefficients of choice models are estimated in units of residual deviation, that is, the coefficient estimates are scaled to allow for the net effect of unobserved factors. When predicting actual choices, we require that these unobserved factors contained in the error term reflect only 'legitimate' influences on actual choices, that is, the influence of those variables not explicitly considered. However, the error term in an SP model will include factors attributable to the SP exercise, such as the difficulties and uncertainties involved with the paper exercise, and these should not be in the model since they do not affect actual behaviour. However, we have no way of isolating these 'illegitimate' effects.

If the residual deviation $(\sigma_{\varepsilon k})$ in a SP model is artificially high due to the error attributable to the SP exercise, it can be seen from equation 4.6 that the scaling factor, Ω, will be too small and hence the coefficient estimates will be too low. The random component of utility will therefore have too much influence and the forecast shares will tend to their equal share values, that is, they will be overestimates (underestimates) for choice probabilities less (greater) than the equal share probability. If the residual deviation is for some reason too small, perhaps because the respondent has ignored the factors (eg. the weather) not in the Stated Preference experiment but which influence actual choices, the forecast shares will tend to their closest extreme values.

Thus the coefficients of SP models may have incorrect scale properties. There are two ways in which this problem might be handled. One method effectively re-scales the SP coefficients by calibrating a logit model which has RP data as the dependent variable and where the independent variables for each alternative k (V_k^{SP}) are utilities constructed on the basis of the SP model's utility weights and the actual travel variables. For the choice between the two modes (1 and 2), such a 'hybrid' model of the logit form would be:

$$P_1 = 1/\{1 + \exp\left[\alpha + \beta\left(V_2^{SP} - V_1^{SP}\right)\right]\} \qquad (4.12)$$

The coefficient β adjusts the SP coefficients to have the same scale properties as the RP model whilst α can adjust for any systematic under/over estimation of particular relative values by the SP model.

However, this implicitly assumes that RP models do not have their own scale factor problem, but measurement error in the independent variables of RP models may mean that the scale properties of the latter are themselves incorrect (Ortuzar and Ivelic, 1987). Alternatively, if we have good information on market share by each mode in known base conditions, it should prove possible to find an adequately good scale factor by choosing that which reconciles the model with this external information. A study by Wardman (1991) finds the consequences of the scale factor to be relatively unimportant but more evidence is required in a variety of different circumstances to allow firmer conclusions to be drawn regarding the extent of this problem for Stated Preference choice models. Current practice seems to be to re-scale SP coefficients according to available evidence on actual behaviour where this is possible, but to use SP models as stand-alone forecasting tools, such as when forecasting the demand for new LRT or rail services, where there is no actual behaviour about which information can be collected. The main alternative, as discussed earlier, is to use the Stated Preference models to give forecasts for individuals and then aggregate to get 'deterministic' forecasts. Clearly various hybrid approaches are also possible.

Transfer Price methods

TP data has a number of attractions in principle. These stem from the rich information content of a response which indicates the strength and not just the order of preference and the fact that it enables the discrete choice demand function with respect to price or some other continuous variable to be fully identified, all else equal. However, TP methods suffer from problems which are typically associated with RP methods, such as measurement error in the independent variables or the lack of a suitable choice context, and also from problems associated with SP methods, such as the responses failing to accurately reflect actual preferences. The difficulty of expressing the strength of a preference is one shortcoming but it seems to be overshadowed by a suspicion that TP questions will be particularly prone to strategic responses.

Such deficiencies, and particularly concerns over the reliability of the responses supplied, to a large extent negate the attractions of the TP method and have meant that it has failed to command widespread appeal. Although Gunn (1984) found a TP model along the lines of equation (4.11) to be capable of recovering similar estimates of the values of in-vehicle time, out-of-vehicle time, walking time and waiting time to a comparable disaggregate logit model based on RP data, there was evidence that the TP responses were seriously understated since the cost coefficient was somewhat less than one. This was in line with Hensher (1976) who reported an example where 75 per cent of respondents did not subsequently change their behaviour in response to a price increase which exceeded their TP response.

4.8 Conclusion

Developments in disaggregate methodologies are continuing,

particularly those concerning Stated Preference techniques. Naturally, it takes some time for the latest developments to become widely known, and even then constraints on time and available expertise may prevent their widespread adoption. Fortunately in the U.K. the new methods have been widely used by the Department of Transport, who accepted their use on their Value of Time Study, British Rail and local authorities, who have used Stated Preference surveys to provide evidence in support of investment projects.

With Stated Preference techniques gaining ever wider acceptance, there is an understandable pressure to apply them in new areas, and for an increasing number of practioners to become involved. We would wish to counsel caution, lest poor applications of SP lead it to fall into disrepute. The design of a completely new SP experiment takes about three months of the time of a suitably experienced analyst, and so is not at all inexpensive. The more that previous designs can be utilised for the new experiment, then the more the design cost falls, until the stage is reached of a simple re-run of a previous design, which obviously takes no fresh design time. The number of practioners having some training and experience with SP is increasing, but the number of published pieces of SP work appears to be falling due to growing constraints of commercial confidentiality.

We would also caution against neglecting possibilities for conducting Revealed Preference surveys. These may be supplemented by Stated Preference questions in order to deal with variables that RP cannot manage, perhaps because of lack of variability in the data. This procedure is particularly sensible when forecasts are required since Stated Preference surveys alone will return parameter estimates incorrectly scaled. While this does not matter when we require relative valuations (such as a value of time) it means that, unless corrected for in some way, forecasts for minority alternatives (eg. modes) are likely to be too high.

One of the other ways of avoiding this last problem is to gather sufficient Stated Preference information about each individual that separate models can be estimated for each. While this will generally require a tediously long pre-planned Stated Preference questionnaire, it is now becoming possible to use computer based Adaptive Stated Preference techniques to cut out irrelevant questions and use early answers to determine subsequent choices to be offered. Obviously this is relatively much more expensive than self completion questionnaires since it requires the provision of a computer and an interviewer. Nevertheless, this is the area of most rapid current development.

56

5 Leisure travel

PHILLIPA MARKS AND MARK WARDMAN

5.1 Introduction and background

Leisure travel accounts for the majority of rail travel outside commuter services. It covers a wide range of specific purposes such as visiting friends and relatives, holidays, shopping, sports and recreation.

This chapter illustrates the use of Stated Preference methods in practice by reporting on two empirical studies of long distance leisure travel by train. The aim of both these studies was to examine leisure travellers' trade-offs amongst various attributes which influence their experiences of and decisions regarding rail travel, and in particular to estimate the money valuations of these attributes. These values can then be used for evaluation purposes, for example, appraising the benefits of rail investments such as faster trains or forecasting behavioural responses to quality and level of service changes.

The first study to be discussed formed part of a larger project whose main objective was to reappraise the value of savings in non-working travel time and which was undertaken for the Department of Transport (MVA, ITS, TSU, 1987). It was concerned with estimating the values of changes to in-vehicle time, service frequency and delay. The second study was undertaken for the InterCity sector of British Rail and examined rail travellers' valuations of various aspects of overcrowding and departure time variations.

Both studies discuss the issues involved in estimating monetary valuations, with particular reference to Stated Preference (SP) methods. The studies provide information on rail travellers' preferences amongst a wide range of travel attributes.

5.2 Methodology of the studies

Both studies used SP methods to estimate relative valuations. Travellers were offered a series of hypothetical travel choices, described in terms of those variables which were of interest, and the responses supplied provide information on the relative importance of these attributes. Both studies work within the conventional economic framework of constrained utility maximisation and use disaggregate methods, where individuals' choices rather than their collective behaviour are the unit of observation. Standard statistical methods are used to estimate and interpret the models of travel choice.

Issues concerning the design of SP experiments and the modelling of responses were discussed in chapter 4. A particular feature of both the studies reported in this chapter is the examination of the effect of socio-economic factors on relative valuations. Both studies used the following common approach. Consider a simple linear-additive utility function containing just time (T) and cost (C).

$$U = \alpha_t T + \alpha_c C \tag{5.1}$$

The usual means of stratification in transport models is to estimate separate models for each category of interest, for example, males and females. As a result, there will be a separate α_t and a separate α_c for males and females. An alternative method (Bates and Roberts, 1986) is to specify dummy variables within a single model to examine whether coefficients vary across different categories of individuals or market segments. These segmented models allow those coefficients which are hypothesised to vary with particular socio-economic factors to do so, whilst all others remain constant. Thus if the sensitivity to travel time is believed to depend on sex, the model would take the form:

$$U = \alpha_t T + \alpha_{tm} d_m T + \alpha_c C \tag{5.2}$$

The dummy variable d_m takes the value 1 if the individual is male, else it is zero. The time coefficient for females is simply α_t whereas the time coefficient for males is α_t plus the incremental term α_{tm}. Determining whether there is a statistically discernable difference between the time coefficients for males and females simply involves testing whether α_{tm} is significantly different from zero.

This approach of specifying dummy variables which interact with the relevant travel variable has the attraction, over calibrating separate models for each category of interest, that the standard errors associated with the estimates are lower because of the increased degrees of freedom.

The segmentation of the model is guided by a priori reasoning. If those with higher incomes are expected to be less sensitive to cost variations, the cost coefficient should be allowed to vary with income. Extending the above equation to allow for variations in the cost coefficient according to three income groups yields:

$$U = \alpha_t T + \alpha_{tm} d_m T + \alpha_c C + \alpha_{ci2} d_{i2} C + \alpha_{ci3} d_{i3} C \qquad (5.3)$$

d_{i2} and d_{i3} are dummy variables representing income groups 2 and 3 respectively. In this case, the base (omitted) category is income group 1 and the incremental coefficients are interpreted in relation to the base category. The extension of the model to allow for other socio-economic factors, for example, the effect of journey purpose as well as sex on the sensitivity to time variations, is straightforward and follows the same principles of specifying incremental terms using dummy variables for n-1 of the n socio-economic categories of interest.

When segmenting a variable by more than one socio-economic factor, eg. allowing the time coefficient to vary with sex and journey purpose, it is possible to allow the effect of sex and purpose to interact with each other, for example, males' sensitivity to time variations is allowed to depend on whether the purpose of the journey is for employer's business, commuting or leisure. In this case of two categories of sex and three of journey purpose, there are six combinations of the two and hence five dummy variables would be specified to allow for all interactions. As the number of variables increases, the number of potential interactions rapidly expands and the examination of the effect of socio-economic factors soon becomes unmanageable with potentially serious consequences for the discriminatory power of the model. Matters are simplified somewhat if the separate effects of the socio-economic variables (for example, purpose and sex) are assumed to be independent of each other, albeit at the potential cost of this convenient simplification being inappropriate. A middle course is to specify those interactions which are considered to be most likely, important or interesting and to take the remaining effects to be additive.

To summarise, there are three main reasons for calibrating segmented models. Firstly, such models at least partially allow for taste variations and thus may produce more accurate estimates than models which pool data across individuals without making any allowance for variations in the parameters across individuals. Secondly, the ability to recover variations in the relative valuations which are consistent with the relationships we would hypothesise to exist allows more faith to be placed in the results derived from the SP data. Finally, the analysis may provide useful information for the purposes of price discrimination and other forms of market segmentation.

5.3 Values of changes in travel time, service frequency and delays for InterCity rail leisure travellers

In this section we report the results of a Stated Preference experiment on InterCity rail leisure travellers. This research was conducted as part of a wider study of the value of travel time savings for public and private transport users for a range of journey purposes conducted for the UK Department of Transport (MVA et al. (1987)). Although the main objectives of this research were to derive travellers' valuations of savings in journey time and to examine how these values varied across different socio-economic groups, we also took the opportunity to include other service characteristics, namely service frequency and reliability (ie. delays) in the experiment.

Data was gathered during June 1985 from on-vehicle surveys of passengers making journeys between the following city pairs: Bristol-London, Manchester-London and Manchester-Birmingham. These routes were chosen to cover a range of journey times (1 to 3 hours) and types of service (Bristol-London is a high quality service, while the Manchester-Birmingham service is a slower stopping service which uses older rolling stock than the other two services). Passengers were screened by journey purpose, to ensure only leisure travellers were included, and journey length, to ensure respondents were making a journey similar to that described in the SP questions. The survey questionnaire asked for information on various socio-economic variables (including age, sex, income and occupation) and on journey characteristics (including journey purpose, ticket type, size of travel party, and time constraints), in addition to asking the respondent to indicate his or her travel preferences in the SP experiment.

The Stated Preference experiment

Survey respondents were asked to consider a hypothetical situation in which they could choose between two different rail services (labelled A and B) for their current journey. As is shown in Table 4.3, one of five possible responses could be given for each pairwise comparison. Respondents were asked to indicate their preferences for twelve such comparisons. A 'within mode' rather than a 'between mode' choice was presented because it was expected that most travellers would have little experience of the other public transport mode (ie. coach) for the journey they were making. This expectation was confirmed; 77 per cent of the sample had not made the relevant journey by coach in the past year.

As Table 4.3 shows, rail services in the SP experiment were described by four attributes: fare, scheduled journey time, service frequency and maximum delay. Fare and journey time were obvious choices and their experimental levels were centred around the then current values for each route. Following Sheldon and Steer (1982) service frequency was portrayed by a timetable of services departing at regular intervals. Finding a simple but meaningful representation of service reliability, however, proved more difficult. Ideally one would want a readily comprehensible (ie. non-statistical) means of describing both the risk and levels of delay (see Benwell and Black (1985), Jackson and Jucker (1981)). It was beyond the scope of our study to develop such a measure. Our approach was to describe reliability in terms of a 'safety margin' (Knight (1974)), that is a maximum delay which respondents were informed could be expected to occur and which they could build into their hypothetical journey plan.

Our starting point in choosing the experimental design was an orthogonal set of comparisons. This was then slightly modified in order that the experiment allowed individuals with a wide range of valuations of the journey attributes to make trade-offs. So that we could check that respondents had answered questions "logically", the experimental design was further modified to include a choice which implied a very low value of time (over a wide range of values for the other attributes) and another which implied a very high value. If a respondent provided answers which revealed both a high and a low value of time, they were classed as having responded illogically and were excluded from the subsequent analysis. Of the 12 binary choices presented, 8 were the orthogonal set, and the remaining 4 implemented the above modifications.

The data

Of the passengers screened into the survey over 80 per cent answered a self-completion questionnaire. From the total 612 returned questionnaires we eliminated those for respondents who either did not answer the SP questions (3 per cent of the total). Those eliminated were more likely to be aged over 55 and retired or in part-time employment than the rest of the sample. In addition, respondents who did not supply data on those socio-economic and journey characteristics which were required in the model estimations were excluded, giving a final sample of 439 respondents (72 per cent of the original sample) and 5,212 SP responses.

The majority of respondents were aged under 35 (approximately 60 per cent), had a household income of less than £10,000 per annum (70%, with 40% having a household income of less than £5,000 per annum). The most important journey purpose was visiting friends and relatives (40 per cent), followed by personal business (16 per cent) and going on holiday (14 per cent). About half the sample were making journeys on the Manchester-London route, another third on the Bristol-London route and the remainder were travelling between Manchester and Birmingham. There were slightly more women in the sample than men.

To analyse the data we assigned each of the five levels of response an ordinal value as follows:

Response	Probability of choosing A
Definitely prefer A	.9
Probably prefer A	.7
Like A and B equally	.5
Probably prefer B	.3
Definitely prefer B	.1

Using these probabilities we estimated the following logit equation using ordinary least squares:

$$\log (p/1-p) = a\ DC + b\ DT + c\ DF + d\ DM + e \qquad (5.4)$$

where p = probability of choosing A
DC = fare A - fare B
DT = journey time A - journey time B

DF = time between services A - time between services B
DM = maximum delay A - maximum delay B
e   = random error

The results

To obtain a preferred model we started with a simple model in which the coefficients of the four explanatory variables (fare, scheduled travel time, frequency and delay) were assumed not to vary systematically across the sample (ie. were assumed constant as in equation (5.4) above). The results are shown in Tables 5.1 and 5.2, and as can be seen the model performs satisfactorily in terms of goodness of fit and significance of the parameter estimates. An average value of in-vehicle time of 5.3 pence per minute was obtained.

The value of changes in the time between services (ie. the service headway) were estimated to be about 2 pence per minute, or about 40 per cent of the value placed on saving a minute of in-vehicle time. This result is consistent British Rail's rule of thumb that the factor used to multiply the service interval to obtain the equivalent journey time equals 0.4. Respondents were found to be highly sensitive to changes in service delays, with a value of 9.3 pence per minute of additional delay being obtained - almost twice the value of scheduled in-vehicle time. This result was not unexpected given the irritation and disruption delays may cause.

Table 5.1
Simple model formulation for rail leisure travel

Variable	Coefficient	(t-ratio)
Cost	-0.00468	(-14.95)
Scheduled time	-0.02492	(-17.40)
Maximum delay	-0.04397	(-17.05)
Headway	-0.00948	(-21.23)

No. of observations = 5,212 R^2 = 37.91%

Note: The t ratios reported here, and elsewhere in this volume, assume that the model errors are independent both within and across individuals, and so should be taken as upper limits.

Table 5.2
Values of time for rail leisure travel from simple model

(pence per minute)

	Value of time	(t-ratio)
Scheduled time	5.32	(12.36)
Maximum delay	9.39	(16.31)
Headway	2.02	(17.56)

Variation in values by traveller characteristics

To investigate whether there was any systematic variation in respondents' valuations of service attributes according to their journey or socio-economic characteristics, we segmented the time and cost variables by these characteristics (allowing for main effects only). A segmentation was retained if it resulted in a significant improvement in model fit (as indicated by the F statistic for the test of restrictions on the coefficients) and gave parameter estimates of the expected sign.

Table 5.3
Values of time for rail leisure travel from segmented model

(pence/minute)

Note: All values apply for lowest income group (<£5,000 per annum), with those for higher income groups obtainable by using the income multipliers at the end of the table.

	Value of time	(t-ratio)
SCHEDULED TIME		
Base	4.34	(10.38)
Incr. for afternoon	-0.74	(-2.87)
MAXIMUM DELAY		
Base	8.65	(11.02)
a. Journey purpose		
Incr. for holiday	-2.92	(-3.67)
Incr. for personal business	+0.46	(+0.62)
Incr. for recreation	-1.81	(-2.69)
Incr. for return home	-2.02	(-3.26)
b. Experience		
Incr. for none	-2.74	(-4.27)
Incr. for 1-5 times	-1.19	(-2.30)

c. Time constraints?		
Incr. for yes	+1.08	(+1.76)
d. Day of week		
Incr. for Friday	+2.03	(+4.33)
e. Income		
Incr. for £5-10,000	-0.48	(-0.57)
Incr. for £10-15,000	-0.22	(-0.21)
Incr. for >£15,000	+1.26	(+1.21)
f. Employment status		
Incr. for student	-2.56	(-3.93)
HEADWAY		
Base	1.85	(10.84)
a. Journey purpose		
Incr. for holiday	-0.25	(-1.80)
Incr. for personal business	+0.14	(+1.06)
Incr. for recreation	-0.34	(-2.72)
Incr. for return home	-0.03	(-0.24)
b. Experience		
Incr. for none	-0.39	(-3.44)
Incr. for 1-5 times	-0.61	(-5.78)
c. Time constraints?		
Incr. for yes	+0.31	(+2.68)
d. Day of week		
Incr. for midweek	+0.37	(-4.21)
e. Income		
Incr. for £5-10,000	+0.29	(+1.72)
Incr. for £10-15,000	+0.21	(+1.08)
Incr. for >£15,000	+0.44	(+2.22)
f. Employment status		
Incr. for student	-0.36	(-2.52)
Incr. for employed	+0.08	(+0.70)
INCOME MULTIPLIERS		
Income £5-10,000	x1.487	
Income £10-15,000	x1.450	
Income £15,000	x1.944	

Table 5.3 gives results for the preferred model. The sensitivity of travellers to the level of fares decreases with income, implying higher values of time for higher income groups. Values of time for the lowest income group (<£5,000 per annum) were significantly less than those for individuals with a household income of £5,000 or more.

We had expected that the value of the coefficient for the journey time variable would depend on the time pressures individuals faced and the flexibility with which they could use their time. On this basis individuals in full-time employment or who care for young children would be expected to have higher journey time coefficient estimates than say either students or retired people. However, contrary to these expectations, the coefficient of the in-vehicle time variable was found to vary only by the time of travel, with a lower value of time being obtained for travel in the afternoon. Although time of travel was found to be significantly correlated with journey purpose (people returning home or visiting friends and relatives were more likely than others to be travelling in the afternoon), segmentation by journey purpose did not result in significant variation in the journey time coefficient.

Estimates of coefficients for the frequency and delay variables, however, were found to vary according to journey purpose, travel experience, the traveller's employment status, whether the traveller was time constrained or not, and the day of travel. Taking each of these segmentations in turn we found that:

- Individuals travelling on personal business or to visit friends and relatives placed higher values on both frequency and delay changes than other categories of leisure travellers (ie. those travelling on holiday, for recreation or returning home). This result could be explained by the fact that those travelling on personal business had to arrive at their destination at a specific time or that people travelling to visit friends and relatives were likely to be met at the station.

- More frequent travellers were more sensitive to changes in frequency and delays than others. This could be because variations in these service attributes have a greater cumulative effect on more frequent travellers' daily time schedules. It is also possible that frequent travellers get more irritated by delays because of past bad experiences with delayed train services. Benwell and Black (1985) found in their study of the reliability of British Rail's services that frequent travellers became more irritated by shorter delays than less frequent travellers.

- Students were less concerned about changes in delays and frequency, possibly reflecting the fact that they have greater flexibility than others in organising their daily time schedules. A similar result might have been expected for the retired but this was not the case. This could be because the retired would be more likely to carefully plan their journeys.

- Time constrained individuals were, as expected, more sensitive to changes in frequency and delays than others. (Individuals were classed as time constrained if they reported having a set arrival time and that it was either impossible or difficult to rearrange their arrival time, as would be the case, for example, if they were catching a plane or were travelling to a doctor's appointment).

- Individuals travelling on a Friday were more sensitive to delays than others, while those travelling mid-week were less sensitive to frequency changes. There is no obvious explanation for these findings other than that we are picking up some aspect of the time constraints people face which is not covered by either the time constraint proxy we used or employment status.

Concluding remarks

The findings presented above indicate that robust value of time estimates can be obtained using data from hypothetical choice experiments. We have most confidence in the estimates obtained for the value of journey time savings. Our estimate of the value of changes in service headway is similar to results obtained in previous studies, while the high estimated value of delays was as we expected. However, that the coefficients of both the service headway and delay variables vary considerably across segments of the sample leads us to suspect that these estimates are less well founded than those for the journey time and cost variables. Service frequency and reliability are much more complex concepts to convey and understand, and it may be that respondents focused largely on the fare and journey time variables in making their choices.

The value of time estimates we obtained are considerably higher than values used by the Department of Transport in valuing travel time savings for road users in cost-benefit analysis. We are not aware of any previous published studies estimating values of time for long distance rail leisure travellers with which we could compare our results. However the value of time study, for which our work was conducted, also included studies which produced value of time estimates for leisure travel by car (short and long distance), coach (long distance) and bus. Estimated values of time for these modes ranged from 1.25 pence per minute for urban bus travel to about 4 pence per minute for long distance coach and car travel, somewhat less than the values we obtained for rail travellers.

MVA et al. (1987) note that, contrary to a priori expectation, the estimated values of time for leisure travellers appear to be inversely correlated with the level of comfort of the travel mode used. The likely explanation offered for this perverse result is sample selection bias. All of the samples in the value of time studies were 'choice based' (that is the sample was chosen on the basis of the travel mode used by the respondents) and it is possible that this has caused them to be biased, in the sense that individuals who choose to travel by a rapid, comfortable, expensive mode may have generally high values of time. If their high value of time is a factor governing their initial mode choice decision, then individuals with high values are more likely to travel by rail than, say, coach or car. We must therefore be careful to interpret our results as applying only to InterCity rail travellers, eg. how much an average InterCity rail traveller would pay to have a 10 minute quicker rail journey, rather than how much an average member of the general public would be prepared to pay to save 10 minutes if they happened to be travelling by rail.

5.4 The values of overcrowding and departure time variations for InterCity rail leisure travellers

The second study to be considered was funded by the British Rail Policy Unit. Interest in the subject arose as a result of increasing overcrowding on popular routes, such as the East Coast Main Line, allied to the fact that relatively little was known about the values passengers placed on reduced overcrowding. Such values are required for the appraisal of investments on routes where overcrowding is a problem and they were also needed as parameter inputs to a model of InterCity operating strategies developed by Galvez-Perez (1989).

The Stated Preference experiment

Self completion questionnaires were sent out in July 1987 to a sample of individuals who had indicated in a recent survey that they would be willing to answer further questions on long distance rail travel. The SP experiment, designed by Tony Fowkes at I.T.S., offered rail travellers sixteen hypothetical travel scenarios based on the train journey they were making when initially contacted. Respondents were required to express a preference between two train options in each scenario on a five point categorical scale denoting either a definite or probable preference for one option or the other or liking/disliking each option equally. The options were described in terms of fare, seating availability and departure time, all other factors being specified to be the same for each option (see Table 4.5).

Fare

This was presented in terms of a variation in the amount actually paid; for example, £5 more, £1 less or no change.

Seating availability

This variable represented four levels of overcrowding, the precise definitions of each being:

Plenty of room (PLENTY)

Those travelling alone would have a bay of four seats to themselves or would have to share with one other person. For those travelling in a group, everyone would be able to sit together in the same bay. In either case, the individual could choose between smoking and no-smoking areas.

Seated but train full (FULL)

The individual would have to share a bay of seats with three other travellers, and groups of travellers would be split up. The respondent was informed that neither he nor any other member of his group would be required to stand but that some other travellers would have to stand at the busiest point. There would be no choice between smoking and no-smoking areas.

Stand for 30 or 60 minutes (STAND30, STAND60)

The train would be full and the individual, or group of travellers, would have to stand either for 30 or for 60 minutes before a seat became available.

Departure time

This variable, referred to as DEPTIME, specified variations in the departure time of the journey. It was included because a possible response to anticipated overcrowding is to change the time of travel. The implied departure time could be the same as for the actual journey made or it could be one or two hours earlier *or* one or two hours later. No individual was presented with both earlier and later departure times. Instead, two separate questionnaires were used to introduce earlier and later departure times and they were randomly distributed to individuals.

The design includes sixteen comparisons, which our experience has shown to be a manageable number. The relevant criteria underlying the design of SP experiments were discussed in Chapter 4 (the illustrative example presented in Table 4.5 is in fact the design used in this study). Suffice to say here that the design process took into account the boundary values implied by the trade-offs introduced and that simulation tests using synthetic data were conducted which showed that the design is capable of accurately recovering a wide range of relative valuations (see Table 4.6).

The data set upon which analysis was conducted includes only: those who purchased standard single/return, saver, day return or executive tickets; those whose journeys were not less than one hour; and those who had supplied information on the time at which their train departed and the time at which they would have most liked to have departed. The latter information allows the analysis of the impact of departure time variations in terms of the implied amount of early and late time involved. The few with journey times of less than one hour were omitted because the SP experiment specified standing for one hour. Ticket types such as free passes/privilege, group, season, and rail rover were omitted due to the special circumstances involved. The remaining sample of leisure travellers contains 393 individuals.

The logit model is most commonly used for analysing discrete choice data and the BLOGIT program (Crittle and Johnson, 1980) was used to explain the (combined definite and probable) preferences between options A and B.

Within leisure travel, a distinction can be made between those who paid their own fare and those whose fare was paid by someone outside the household. The data set contains 282 of the former and 111 of the latter. The main analysis was conducted on those leisure travellers who paid their own fare and the calibrated model for these individuals is presented in Table 5.4.

Results for leisure travellers who paid their own fare

The representative utility function contains early time (EARLY), late time (LATE), the amount of time seated in a full train (FULL), whether standing for 30 minutes (STAND30) was required, whether standing for 60 minutes (STAND60) was required and the cost. The coefficients are assumed to have the same value for both options since there is no reason why they should vary by option in this exercise. The variables can therefore be specified in difference form in this binary choice context. Although the unit value of standing time is allowed to vary between 30 and 60 minutes standing time, FULL, EARLY and LATE have constant unit values in the model.

Table 5.4
Leisure travellers who paid their own fare

Coefficient of EARLY	-0.0135	(10.11)
Coefficient of LATE	-0.0148	(11.18)
Coefficient of FULL	-0.0026	(7.61)
Coefficient of STAND30	-1.8657	(21.31)
Coefficient of STAND60	-2.1926	(14.71)
Coefficient of COST	-0.0030	(16.63)
t (EARLY-LATE)	0.78	
VALUE OF EARLY (p/min)	4.50	(10.49)
VALUE OF LATE (p/min)	4.93	(11.77)
VALUE OF FULL (p/min)	0.87	(7.98)
VALUE OF STAND30	£6.22	(18.74)
VALUE OF STAND60	£7.31	(25.02)
RHO BAR SQUARED	0.20	
OBSERVATIONS	3271	
INDIVIDUALS	282	

Note: t ratios in brackets

Early (late) time represents a departure before (after) the desired time. If option A requires a one hour earlier departure than for the actual journey made, and the individual travelled 30 minutes earlier than desired, the early time associated with option A is 90 minutes. Given that option B does not vary the departure time, it would involve the actual amount of early time of 30 minutes. Late time would be zero for both options. If instead option A introduced a departure time one hour later than for the actual journey, option A now incurs 30 minutes late time whilst option B, which has not changed, involves the 30 minutes early time of the actual journey. Although a departure time variation which moves the individual closer to the desired departure time will generally be beneficial, any amount of early or late time incurs disutility. The estimated values of early and late time represent the disutility in money terms of having to depart one minute earlier/later than desired.

It was possible to calibrate a satisfactory SP model for leisure travellers who paid their own fare. The coefficients are all of the correct sign, denoting that more of any of the variables reduces utility, and they are all highly significant. However, there is currently some debate about the status of the error term in SP models due to individuals undertaking multiple evaluations of travel options. This has been termed the repeat observations problem. The model assumes that the errors are independent both within and across individuals. It has been argued that the errors within an individual's responses may be correlated and that each response does not constitute a separate piece of information. A 'conservative' correction would be to multiply the standard errors of the estimates by the square root of the number of choices made by each individual. This would only be correct if there were perfect correlation with each individual's responses and would thus most certainly be an over-adjustment. However, it at least gives an upper bound to the standard errors. No allowance has been made in the reported model for the repeat observations problem. Since the model contains 282 individuals, there are, on average, 11.6 observations per person. As a rough correction, and assuming the worst case of perfect correlation, the t ratios could be deflated by 3.4. The estimated coefficients and relative values remain significant, and generally highly significant, when this is done.

The estimated model is satisfactory in terms of the goodness of fit achieved. Hensher and Johnson (1979, p.51) state, 'It should be noted, however, that values of Rho Squared of between 0.2 and 0.4 are considered extremely good fits so that the analyst should not be looking for values in excess of 0.9 as is often the case when using R^2 in ordinary regression'.

The relationship between the values of EARLY and LATE is likely to depend on a number of factors and remains to be empirically determined. It could be argued that LATE time will be relatively highly valued because of attendance at an appointment or event with a fixed starting time or because the amount of time that can be spent at the destination is reduced. On the other hand, the inconvenience of getting up earlier or arriving too early and incurring idle time may lead to a relatively high value of EARLY.

The EARLY and LATE coefficients are not significantly different from each other (t = 0.78) and, according to statistical criteria, the two could be combined into a single variable to represent the effect of variations from the ideal departure time. The other models calibrated, for leisure travellers whose fare is paid by someone outside the household and for business travellers, also found late time to be only slightly more highly valued than early time. Analysis was conducted to examine whether the values of EARLY/LATE varied with the amount of early/late time but no clear trend emerged and therefore the constant unit value form was maintained.

The values of EARLY and LATE are slightly less than the value of in-vehicle time reported in section 5.3 above for InterCity leisure travellers. This suggests that individuals would regard favourably the opportunity to 'purchase' a given amount of travel time saving

72

by increasing their early or late time by a corresponding amount.

The relationships between the overcrowding values are consistent. The value of STAND60 exceeds the value of STAND30, the value of standing time exceeds the value of time spent seated and the value of time spent seated exceeds the value of time spent in the base situation where there is plenty of room. Individuals may be averse to having to stand at all, for example, because there is a feeling that standing should not be necessary, or there may be some fixed penalty involved in finding a good standing place. Such an effect could be represented by a dummy variable denoting whether standing was required. The unit value of standing might also be expected to increase with the amount of standing time as 'thresholds of bearability' are passed. However, it is not possible to separately identify a fixed penalty associated with having to stand and a non-constant unit value of standing time because there are only two levels of standing time in this experiment.

The unit value of standing time is 20.73 pence per minute in the range up to 30 minutes, which is very much larger than the 3.63 pence per minute in the 30 to 60 minute range. These results do suggest that there is a fixed penalty involved in standing, a result which has been confirmed in subsequent studies. Interpreting the results in terms of a fixed penalty and a constant value of standing time, leisure travellers would require £5.13 to compensate them for having to stand (higher values were found for business travellers, and for leisure travellers who were not themselves paying for the journey). The implied fixed penalty does seem to be rather high, and it would need to be even higher to be consistent with an increasing unit value of standing time. Further research is required with additional levels of standing time to examine in more detail the issues surrounding the value of avoiding the need to stand and the relationship between the value and amount of standing time.

One thing which is clear is that reductions in overcrowding are highly valued. Changing the departure time and incurring an additional hour of early or late time would on average be valued at less than £3 and would seem to be a particularly attractive option if it meant that standing for either 30 or 60 minutes could be avoided. Similarly, travellers would be prepared to tolerate somewhat longer journey times if standing could be avoided.

Variations in relative values according to socio-economic factors

Analysis was conducted to examine variations in the values of EARLY/LATE, FULL, STAND30 and STAND60 according to socio-economic factors. This was done for leisure travellers who paid their own fare. The segmentation procedure used was that of specifying dummy variable interaction terms as outlined in Section 5.2 above. Instead of initially entering all the socio-economic variables into a single model, a number of relatively simple segmented models containing at most only two socio-economic variables were first calibrated. Once some indication was obtained of which variables had more than a negligible influence, more complete models containing these variables were calibrated.

The variables which were considered in the process of developing a preferred segmented model were gross household income, age, sex, class of travel, group travel, journey purpose, journey time and departure time. The final model is reported in Table 5.5.

Since the coefficients of EARLY and LATE were previously found to be similar and insignificantly different, they have been combined into a variable (DT) which represents divergences from the desired departure time. The coefficient values for DT, FULL, STAND30 and STAND60 are interpreted in an absolute sense and the remaining coefficient values represent incremental effects attributable to a particular category of a socio-economic variable. The omitted category of these variables (BASE) is shown for clarity. A separate cost coefficient was estimated for each of the four income groups and thus each of the cost coefficients can be taken to be an absolute value. This is entirely equivalent to specifying a cost variable for all individuals and three incremental cost variables to represent all but one of the income groups.

The specification of the model assumes interactions between socio-economic variables to be negligible and therefore the effects of each can simply be added. As an example of how to interpret the model, consider the maximum and minimum values which can be obtained from the model:

	DT	FULL	STAND30	STAND60
MAXIMUM	8.65	3.30	£18.05	£27.15
MINIMUM	2.28	0.55	£1.64	£1.88

The maximum value of STAND30 (and also of STAND60) is for those travelling first class who are female, aged over 60, making journeys of over three hours and who are in the highest income group. The value of STAND30 for this group is calculated as:

$$(-1.0835 - 0.9482 - 0.2825 - 0.6403 - 1.1967)/(-0.0023) = £18.05$$

Table 5.5
Segmented model for leisure travellers paying their own fare

DT	-0.0151	(13.43)	
No Children		BASE	
With Children	-0.0048	(1.99)	(30% Higher)
FULL	-0.0036	(9.43)	
2nd Class		BASE	
1st Class	-0.0040	(2.04)	(100% Higher)
STAND30	-1.0835	(6.92)	
2nd Class		BASE	
1st Class	-0.9482	(1.87)	(90% Higher)
Male		BASE	
Female	-0.2825	(2.10)	(25% Higher)
Time 1-2 Hours		BASE	
Time 2-3 Hours	-0.4631	(2.93)	(40% Higher)
Time 3+ Hours	-0.6403	(3.17)	(60% Higher)
Age 16-24		BASE	
Age 25-59	-0.6147	(3.37)	(60% Higher)
Age 60+	-1.1967	(4.73)	(110% Higher)
STAND60	-1.2450	(3.98)	
2nd Class		BASE	
1st Class	-0.9376	(1.71)	(75% Higher)
Male		BASE	
Female	-0.7386	(4.73)	(60% Higher)
Time 1-2 Hours		BASE	
Time 2-3 Hours	-0.5180	(2.49)	(40% Higher)
Time 3+ Hours	-1.1943	(5.44)	(100% Higher)
Age 16-24		BASE	
Age 25-59	-1.0780	(6.06)	(90% Higher)
Age 60+	-2.1292	(7.75)	(170% Higher)
COST			
Income < £5000	-0.0066	(14.02)	
Income £5-15000	-0.0044	(15.10)	(All Values 50% Higher)
Income £15-20000	-0.0037	(11.60)	(All Values 80% Higher)
Income £20000+	-0.0023	(9.88)	(All Values 190% Higher)
RHO BAR SQUARED	0.25		

Note: Approximate proportionate effects in relation to the base category are given in the final column.

The minimum value of STAND30 is for the base category, that is the absolute coefficient for STAND30, and the lowest income group and is therefore calculated as:

$$-1.0835/-0.0066 = £1.64$$

The incremental effects in the model presented should all have negative signs because the effect of any of these variables is expected to increase the values of DT, FULL, STAND30 and STAND60. The coefficient estimates are therefore all of the expected sign. Most coefficients are statistically significant, the remaining ones being only marginally insignificant.

Those with higher incomes are likely to be less sensitive to cost variations and thus they will have lower cost coefficients. A strong monotonic income effect of the expected form is apparent and the four cost coefficients are significantly different from each other. Those with the highest incomes have relative values which are around three times greater than for those with the lowest incomes.

There is a particularly strong effect from class of travel on the sensitivity to overcrowding. The value of FULL for first class travellers is double that of second class travellers, *ceteris paribus*, whilst the values of STAND30 and STAND60 are 88 per cent and 75 per cent higher respectively for first class travellers. These findings are not surprising. Those travelling first class can be expected to be more averse to full trains and to having to stand because it is likely that one of the reasons underlying their decision to travel first class is that it is less crowded.

Age emerged as another strong effect. The value of STAND30 for those 60 and over is slightly more than twice that for the youngest age group whilst the corresponding increase in the value of STAND60 is 171 per cent. The elderly can reasonably be expected to be more averse to standing, although there is less reason to expect them to be much more averse to a full train than other travellers. Those in the 25-44 and 45-59 age group had similar coefficients for STAND30 and STAND60 but they were higher than for the 16-24 age group. The FULL coefficient hardly varied across age groups.

The segmentation of the overcrowding variables showed that females had somewhat higher values of standing than males, particularly STAND60 which is around 60 per cent higher. There was little difference in the values of FULL for males and females.

The unit value of time spent seated in a full train appeared to be essentially constant with respect to the amount of travel time. However, there was a strong tendency for the values of STAND30 and STAND60 to increase with the actual journey time. The values of STAND30 and STAND60 both increase by around 40 per cent when journey time increases from the base level of 1-2 hours to 2-3 hours whilst journeys of over 3 hours have a value of STAND30 60 per cent greater than the base category and a value of STAND60 which, at 96 per cent higher, is one of the strongest effects apparent in the model. The relationships between the values of standing time and the actual journey time seem reasonable.

Those travelling in groups are likely to suffer more as a result of a FULL train since it was specified that the group would be split up in such instances. Those travelling with children may find a train journey which involves standing especially arduous. It came as a surprise, therefore, that there were hardly any differences in the FULL, STAND30 and STAND60 coefficients according to whether the respondent was travelling in a group or not and whether there were any children in the group.

Journey purpose is often used as a classificatory variable and the study distinguished between business and leisure travel. Whilst some variations in the overcrowding coefficients due to journey purpose were apparent, they were not considered to be sufficiently strong to merit inclusion in a more complete model.

The discussion so far has related to the segmentations of the overcrowding variables. The values of EARLY and LATE are expected to be influenced by fewer socio-economic variables than was the case for the values of the overcrowding variables. Although first and second class differ in terms of comfort, and thus can be used to segment individuals according to the value they place on overcrowding, travelling first class does not yield any benefits in terms of departure times. Nor does there seem to be any strong reason why the values of early/late time should vary according to age or sex. The factors about which data was collected and which were considered to be most likely to influence the sensitivity to DT variations were the actual departure time, journey purpose and group travel.

The value of early time may well be different for earlier departures since the individual may have to get up earlier than otherwise and this may have a relatively high disutility. Similarly, late time may be relatively highly valued for journeys which are made late during the day and where the arrival time at the destination would be regarded as being too late. The values of EARLY and LATE were separately segmented according to departure time but the effects were far from significant.

It would seem more likely that the values of early/late time vary with journey purpose than do the values of the overcrowding variables. Journey purpose can, to some extent, proxy for the time constraints which may influence the value of early/late time; for example, those travelling on personal business are often attending events or appointments with a fixed starting time and thus EARLY may be relatively highly valued, because of the idle time involved, whilst LATE may also be highly valued if arriving late incurs a penalty. However, there were again no significant influences on the sensitivity to variations in DT.

It could be argued that not being able to travel at the desired time has a greater disutility for those travelling in a group. Those travelling with children may find the inconvenience of having to depart earlier to be greater than for those who are travelling alone. Similarly, the value of late time may be relatively high if it is desired that the children are home for a particular time. For other groups of travellers, there may be the inconvenience of re-arranging travel patterns or group travel may no longer be feasible. DT was segmented according to whether the respondent was travelling alone or not and, if not, whether there were any children in the group. There was an effect arising from travelling with children but none attributable to whether the individual was travelling in a group containing adults only. Thus the final model simply distinguishes between those travelling with and without children, the former valuing DT around 30 per cent higher than the latter.

5.5   Conclusion

It has been possible to calibrate SP models for leisure travellers which achieve satisfactory goodness of fit and which have coefficients which are of the correct sign and generally highly significant. These models exhibit variations in the relative valuations according to a number of socio-economic variables. The estimated effects of the socio-economic variables are consistent with expectations and their absolute magnitudes seem reasonable, for example, the effect attributable to the elderly was one of the most pronounced in the model in relation to standing time. Although the results for the segmentations of schedule delay (DT) are perhaps disappointing, data was not collected on factors such as arrival and departure constraints and penalties which could be expected to exert a strong influence on the value of DT. Overall, the results of the SP models, and particularly the segmentation results, are encouraging with regard to the validity of SP data and methods.

6 Business travel

TONY FOWKES, PHILLIPA MARKS AND CHRIS NASH

6.1   Introduction

The usual definition of business travel is 'travel in the course of work'; it thus includes much more than just the traditional 'briefcase' traveller or 'businessman'. What makes this form of travel particularly difficult to analyse is the mix of individual and organisation incentives involved in planning the journey.   For instance, we might think of two extremes of circumstances under which the journey is planned. In the first, the company - either through a tightly defined travel policy or through the decisions of a manager in charge of company travel, dictates exactly what journeys are to be made, what modes to be used and so on. In this case we might analyse travel decisions in much the same way as we have in previous chapters for other journey purposes, but we must be aware that it is the preferences of the organisation we are measuring, not those of the individual making the journey. In the second case, the organisation leaves complete discretion to the individual making the journey.   In this case, it will be the preferences of the individual which determine the decisions taken, but in the particular circumstances that he or she does not have to bear the financial costs.   Thus we might expect them simply to choose the mode which they regard as offering the highest quality in the circumstances in question.   In practice, it seems from the evidence that even when they do not have to bear the costs, business travellers do take some account of the cost to the company of their decisions, possibly in order to earn 'brownie' points from their superiors.

In reality the situation appears rarely to be at either extreme. It will be seen below that most organisations allow the traveller a degree of discretion within an overall travel policy. Thus, observed decisions are a mixture of the choices of individual and organisation. Moreover, the circumstances surrounding the reimbursement of costs introduce complications of their own. Firstly, travel expenditure is usually tax deductible, so companies have an incentive to be generous in this respect as a cheaper way of enhancing their employment remuneration package than by a salary increase. The most obvious manifestation of this tendency is the widespread provision of company cars (TEST, 1984). Once a company car has been provided as a perk, there is then an incentive to use it, partly because for the company the marginal cost of its use may be low relative to other modes, and also for the individual, who must achieve a certain mileage on company business to avoid being taxed on the value of a car as a perk.

Where a company car is not used, the method of reimbursement may influence mode choice decisions as well. For instance a company may pay first class rail fares, in order to ensure that their staff have the status, comfort and ability to work which go with travelling first class. However, if it does not check on the mode actually used, staff may travel standard class, or by car, and retain the difference in cost. Where companies reimburse staff for the use of their own car, much will depend on whether staff see the mileage rate paid as more, or less than the marginal cost to them of using the car. If they see the rate as generous, then they have an incentive to use the car, and cover some of their own fixed costs at the company's expense. If it is seen as inadequate, then they will feel that they are subsidising their employer by using their own car, and will try to avoid doing so.

It follows from this that a study of business travel should try to understand company travel and reimbursement policies; what may make them change; and the preferences of individuals when travelling on business from amongst the choice set open to them. We should also note that when an individual is travelling, alone, to a meeting for which he or she needs to prepare on the way and needs to perform well on arrival, their own individual preferences may well be different from when they are out on a leisure trip with their family.

In 1985-86, the Institute undertook a major study of Business

Travel, financed by the Science and Engineering Research Council. The results of that study form the basis of this chapter. Fuller details are available in Fowkes and Marks (1985), Fowkes, Johnson and Marks (1985), Fowkes, Marks and Nash (1986), Marks (1986a) and Marks, Fowkes and Nash (1986). The main purpose of the study was to examine the appropriate value of time to use for business travellers in economic evaluations. The study also threw some light on the travel behaviour of business travellers. In the next section we consider the results of a survey of organisations regarding their travel policies. We then consider the determinants of mode choice, looking both at the most recent trip undertaken by respondents, and at stated preferences both by themselves and their employers as to their willingness to pay to save time on the journey.

6.2   Company travel policies

As part of the above mentioned study, we undertook a telephone survey of the policies of 311 organisations in Greater London and Tyne and Wear (the former was chosen because of its importance in the world of business travel and the latter because its distance from London gave a finely balanced choice of rail or air for trips to that destination, with car also possible and likely to dominate to other destinations). The stratified sample was designed to provide evidence on a wide range of types and sizes of organisation; details are given in Table 6.1.

We first distinguish between formal travel policies, with clearly written rules, informal travel policies and those organisations which claimed to have no travel policy at all. Altogether, 83 per cent of organisations had either a formal or informal travel policy (Table 6.2). Public establishments are more likely to have a travel policy than private, and this is also more likely to be formal. Not surprisingly, there is also a greater likelihood of having a travel policy, the larger the organisation. It is also the case that in larger organisations, the company is more likely to decide the mode of travel for business trips, whereas in smaller organisations it is more likely to be the individual making the journey who decides. Regarding reimbursement, a variety of methods was in use, with some firms paying actual travel costs (sometimes checking expenditure by providing travel warrants or specific credit cards for the purpose) and others reimbursing at the level of first or standard class rail fare, or a mileage rate for car.

Table 6.1
Details of the sample of organisations

(a)   Distribution of Greater London sample by size and industry type

----------------------------Type----------------------------

Size	Public Non-Comm.	Public Comm.	Prof. Service	Light Indus.	Heavy Indus.	Other	TOTAL
1-10	1	-	10	3	5	5	24
11-20	-	-	6	4	4	1	15
21-50	2	1	6	10	4	3	26
51-100	1	-	3	5	6	1	16
101-200	2	2	11	3	7	7	32
201-500	3	1	5	11	2	2	24
500-1000	-	1	2	1	2	-	6
1001+	2	2	4	-	-	-	8
Total	11	7	47	37	30	19	151

(b)   Distribution of North East sample by size and industry type

----------------------------Type----------------------------

Size	Public Non-Comm.	Public Comm.	Prof. Service	Light Indus.	Heavy Indus.	Other	TOTAL
1-10	2	-	11	-	3	1	17
11-20	4	1	3	4	7	3	22
21-50	1	1	11	4	9	6	32
51-100	-	2	5	4	7	3	21
101-200	-	2	-	7	9	3	21
201-500	1	2	4	6	8	1	22
501-1000	7	2	-	1	1	-	11
Total	15	12	35	34	47	17	160

Note: unabreviated headings are shown in Table 6.2

We asked organisations if they had changed their travel policies recently, or if they had plans to do so in the near future. A total of 69 recent changes and 13 planned changes were reported, but there was little systematic about them, except that in the depressed business conditions at the time of the survey there tended to be a cost cutting flavour about many of them.   For instance 10 organisations had reduced their use of first class rail travel, whilst

5 had switched to smaller cars. Several were undertaking less travel, and some were paying lower mileage allowances. It would be interesting to know the extent to which these decisions were reversed in the ensuing business upswing.

Table 6.2
Travel policy by establishment type

(Percentage responding. Median establishment size in brackets)

	Formal	Informal	None
Public Non-commercial	81 (201-500)	15 (21-50)	4 (1-10)
Public Commercial	58 (501-1000)	32 (101-200)	5 (51-100)
Professional Services	33 (51-100)	50 (21-50)	15 (1-10)
Light Industry	24 (201-500)	55 (51-100)	20 (21-50)
Heavy Industry	21 (101-200)	58 (51-100)	20 (11-20)
Other	25 (101-200)	44 (21-50)	28 (51-100)
Total	33 (101-200)	50 (51-100)	17 (21-50)

88 per cent of organisations gave at least one member of their staff a company car, with those that did not being mainly public sector organisations. Of those organisations providing company cars, approximately half stated that holders of company cars were expected to use them for most or all long distance journeys. Where a company car was not provided or not expected to be used, the permitted modes of travel for which expenses would be reimbursed were as in Table 6.3. Not surprisingly, reimbursement for travel by air or first class rail is mainly confined to senior and middle management; for all categories of staff, companies are more willing to reimburse rail fares than the mileage rate for staff using their own car.

The results of this section of the work confirmed that there was a wide variety of travel policies and reimbursement decisions in existence, many of which left considerable - but not complete - discretion open to the individual. Clearly, disentangling the motives behind individual travel decisions would be complicated. For this reason, as well as the fact that many choices appeared to be dominated, with either rail (for journeys to London) or car (for other journeys) being the obvious mode, we undertook Stated Preference surveys both of individuals and of managers responsible for company travel policy. But first we report on the actual journeys made by a sample of respondents.

Table 6.3
Percentage of establishments reimbursing
staff for business travel by transport mode

	Air	1st Class Rail	All Rail	Own Car
Senior Mgt.	86	64	91	39
Middle Mgt.	60	31	69	36
Junior Mgt.	21	8	27	15
Secretarial/Clerical	8	1	13	11
Technical	24	9	32	18
Manual	5	1	6	5

6.3 Actual travel behaviour

We also distributed questionnaires to employees of the organisations discussed in the previous section, asking them for details of their most recent long distance (i.e. over 50 miles) business trip. A similar sample of travellers was drawn from a survey of rail passengers on the East Coast Main Line (ECML). Results for these respondents are not given in this chapter, but are very similar in all main respects to those now to be presented.

Altogether, usable replies were received from 442 people, of whom rather more than half were in managerial positions, the remainder being almost entirely professional or technical staff. Of these, 48 per cent had used car for their most recent trip, 38 per cent rail and the remainder air. A very small number of people used a different mode for their return journey. There was a much higher probability of having used car amongst those with a company car (62 per cent as opposed to 38 per cent of those without a company car). There was also a greater tendency to use car when visiting clients than when travelling for other purposes.

Of course, both of these findings may be a result of the ease of access to the destination of the trip. The reasons for the journeys are listed in Table 6.4. The predominant reason was visiting clients, but attending conferences came second in frequency.

Table 6.4
Purpose of meetings held on last business trip by
outward journey main mode

(per cent of meetings by mode)

Purpose	Car	Train	Air	All
Visit Head Office	-	3	2	1
Visit Branch Site	11	9	8	10
Visit Client	42	24	36	36
Attend Conference	9	29	18	17
Attend T.U. Meeting	-	-	-	-
Demonstrate Goods	1	5	-	3
Other	34	30	36	33
Total no. of meetings	217	124	52	393

When we look at the modes of transport permitted to the various occupations (Table 6.5) we find that most people were permitted a choice of rail or car. However, only about half of the respondents would be allowed to use first class on rail (these were mainly managerial and professional workers), and it appears that some technical staff were required to use car rather than rail. Use of air is more tightly controlled than use of first class rail.

Table 6.5
Permitted modes by occupation

(% respondents for each occupation category)

	Managerial	Professional	Technical	Other	Total
Car	83	83	93	90	85
Rail (1st)	57	63	38	30	55
Rail (Std)	86	90	73	85	85
Air	48	47	34	25	45
Coach	29	36	25	40	31
Respondents	250	111	56	20	437

Reasons given for the modes actually chosen are listed in Table 6.6. Whilst it is clear that obtaining the shortest possible journey time is the most important consideration, the ability to depart at a convenient time is also frequently cited (and of course particularly favours car), whilst about a third of those using rail mentioned the ability to work on the train as a factor. Only a small proportion of our sample were constrained to the use of car by the need to carry equipment.

Table 6.6
Reasons for choice of main means of travel
for the outward journey*

(% respondents for each mode mentioning the reason indicated)

Reason	Car	Train	Air	All
Cheapest	23	19	5	19
Company policy	29	33	5	27
Convenient start-time	40	35	33	37
Short journey time	31	44	95	43
Able to work on journey	3	34	-	14
Need to carry equipment	14	-	3	7
Other	37	24	14	29
No. of respondents	207	162	64	433

* NB: the distribution of reasons for the mode chosen on the return journey is very similar to that shown here for the outward journey.

6.4   Stated Preference experiments - employers

In order to examine the likely effects on business travel of a change in the price or quality of a particular mode, it is necessary to examine the reaction both of employers and of the travellers themselves. We thus conducted two simple Stated Preference exercises. The first, and most simple (because it had to be administered over the telephone) was that asked of the managers interviewed as being responsible for their organisation's travel policy. The question asked was this:

'Now suppose a first class only premium accelerated rail service between London and Newcastle was introduced, saving one hour's travel time on the round trip, compared with their usual means of travel. Would senior staff be allowed to use the service if the extra cost was £5... was £20... was £50? And what about other staff?'

For the two types of staff, this question gives the proportion of establishments whose value of time falls into each of the ranges 0 to £5, £5 to £20, £20 to £50, and over £50. We plotted the cumulative frequency against the value of time, and then used linear interpolation to estimate the median value of time for each group. Results are shown in table 6.7. The result is a very high value of time of £16 per hour (early 1984 prices) for senior staff compared with £6 per hour for other staff.

Table 6.7
Median values of time (£/hour) (early 1984)

	Senior Staff	Other Staff	Sample Size
Total Sample	16	6	311
Public Non-commercial	9	4	26
Public Commercial	22	10	19
Professional	18	6	82
Light Industry	15	9	71
Heavy Industry	15	6	77
Other	13	6	36
1-50 employees	13	4	136
51-500 employees	16	8	136
501+ employees	28	9	39

We also asked about typical salaries of the staff in question, from which it emerged that senior staff were paid about £9 per hour, whilst other staff were paid about half this much. (It should be noted that these calculations are based on normal working hours; if senior staff actually worked much longer hours, then the hourly rate would be correspondingly lower). However, to estimate the cost to the employer of an hour's time of the person in question, we have to add on National Insurance, superannuation, other overheads and the cost of fringe benefits. It appeared that these would add at least a further 40 per cent in the case of senior staff, but rather less than this for other staff (Royal Commission on the Distribution of Income and Wealth, 1976).

In other words, it appeared that employers willingness to pay to save staff time exceeded the cost to them of that time, although not by a very great margin. Neoclassical theory would, of course, lead us to expect the two to be the same. However, in the case of the sort of staff and journeys that we are talking about, we would not necessarily expect a close coincidence between the two. Firstly, staff were typically starting journeys in the early morning in their own time, and were able to work on the journey. In the survey of travellers, we asked for the amount of time they spent working whilst travelling, and for train travellers this averaged nearly an hour on the outward journey and half an hour on the return. Secondly, we also asked what they would have done with the time saved if the journey could have started later, and the responses split almost equally between working and staying in bed.

Both these factors would lead us to expect the employer to be willing to pay less than the hourly cost of staff to save travel time. On the other hand, employers presumably have an interest in staff arriving at meetings rested and well prepared for the business at hand, and there is also an element of prestige and of salary enhancement regarding the provision of travel expenses. Thus it may just be coincidence that the employers willingness to pay is not so far removed from the hourly cost of staff.

6.5   Stated Preference experiments - business travellers

We now turn to the experiments we conducted to see how business travellers valued their own travel time. These were conducted by means of the self completion questionnaire administered both to people contacted through the organisations (ORGN) and to rail travellers intercepted on the East Coast Main Line (ECML). The aim was to put travellers in a position where they would essentially be paying the extra costs of a superior mode of travel out of their own pocket (in other words, corresponding to the situation where they can claim a fixed allowance, but there is no control on the mode they actually use).

We therefore told respondents that they would be required to make a return journey from Newcastle to London in the course of a day, with a free choice of whether to travel by air, first class rail, second (standard) class rail or to drive. They would be paid a fixed expense allowance of £100, and would be free to keep any unspent money. They were then presented with twelve ranking tasks, in each of which they were given the round trip travel cost, departure time from home and arrival time back at home for each of the four modes.

It was hoped that respondents would answer the ranking exercise by trading differences in cost against differences in time away from home, the inconvenience of start times and any other perceived differences between the services offered by the four modes. The experiment was designed by setting the start times and total times, which together determined the finish times. Levels of the time and cost variables were chosen so that the data would identify a reasonably wide range of time valuations. An orthogonal design was not considered possible because of the constraints imposed by the following 'real life' considerations:

(i)   Travel times by first and second class rail should be equal, unless we were to complicate the analysis by having frequent first class only trains.

(ii)   The cost of first class rail should be about 50 per cent greater than the cost of second class rail, as is usually the case during the business peak. As in (i) we wished to keep our hypothetical options as close as possible to travellers' actual experiences.

In order to ensure the experiment could identify a wide range of values of time, 'boundary' values of time were calculated for each modal comparison (see Section 4.5). A 'boundary' value of time is the value of time at which an individual would be indifferent between a given pair of modes. The intention was to allow for a wide range of in-vehicle values of time, together with a wide range of variability in valuations of factors other than cost and time. The effect of these other factors is captured by Alternative Specific Constants (ASC's) included in model calibrations, where they represent the utility gain (or loss) of, say, flying as opposed to travelling by first class rail, assuming the costs and times are identical for both modes. Attribute values were primarily chosen so that choices between air, and first and second class rail covered a wide range of boundary values of time. Travel by car was not expected to be a serious option for most respondents because of the length of the hypothetical journey.

Before analysing the ranking data we first checked whether the respondents answered the experiment 'sensibly' and whether they traded off cost and time, or ranked modes on the basis of only one of these attributes. We checked the data for occurrences of inconsistent choices and found only 4 in each sample. These people were excluded from the data used in model estimations reported in the next section.

The data from the ranking exercise will clearly be of little value if a large proportion of respondents did not trade off time and cost when deciding their rankings. We were, therefore, interested to find out how many people appeared to:

(i)   Always rank modes on the basis of time alone, i.e. had a very high value of time;

(ii)   Always rank modes on the basis of cost alone, i.e. had a very low value of time;

(iii) Always gave the same ranking, i.e. considered attributes other than time and cost to be overwhelmingly important.

As table 6.8 shows none of the ECML and only 6 of the ORGN sample gave rankings on the basis of only cost or time. This suggests the experimental design was adequate, in this respect.

Table 6.8
Number of 'non-trading' respondents

	Order on cost alone*	Order on time alone*	Same rankings*
ECML	-	-	18
ORGN	1	5	30

* Only respondents with 2 or more sets of rankings were counted here.

However, 18 of the ECML and 30 of the ORGN respondents gave the same ordering of modes for all of the ranking exercises they answered. Looking in more detail at this data we found that in each sample approximately half of these respondents gave the ranking 1234 (i.e. air = 1, 1st rail = 2, 2nd rail = 3, car = 4). One could either interpret this as meaning cost considerations are dominated by the value placed on short journey time and comfort, or that these people did not take the ranking exercise seriously and always wrote down the most obvious answer, i.e. 1234. Some support for the former explanation comes from the observation that a relatively large proportion of respondents who always answered 1234 earned £20,000 or more per annum (43 per cent compared with 25 per cent in the complete ECML sample and 15 per cent in the complete ORGN sample). Nevertheless, we decided to remove respondents who always gave the same answer from the sample because it was still not clear they had taken the ranking exercise seriously. Removing these respondents from the sample resulted in a slight reduction in the value of time estimates.

90

To summarise, almost all respondents from both samples appear to have answered the Stated Preference exercise as was intended, with time and cost attributes being traded and with very few irrational choices being made. Responses thought likely to have arisen other than in the expected way have been removed from the data used for model calibrations.

Results

The exploded logit technique was used to analyse the ranked data (Chapman and Staelin (1982)). The software used to perform the estimations was an augmented version of the Australian Research Board's Basic Logit (BLOGIT) package (Crittle and Johnson (1980)). Because this package uses a large amount of disk space when analysing ranked data, we were only able to perform estimations on subsets of each of the ORGN and ECML samples. From each sample we drew a random subset comprising the Stated Preference answers of every second respondent who gave 'rational' rankings, and who supplied income and occupation data. Separate models were estimated for the ECML and ORGN subsamples.

Searching for an appropriate model specification, we started with a simple time and cost model and added variables which gave a statistically significant improvement in the fit of the model, at the 5 per cent level. To perform this test we used the Chi-squared test statistic for nested models i.e. $2 \, (LL(M_k) - LL(M_{k+1}))$

where

M_k	=	model with k explanatory variables
M_{k+1}	=	model with k+1 explanatory variables
LL(M)	=	log-likelihood of model M

The variables we first considered adding to the model were the early morning start dummies E1, E2, E3 and E4 where:

E1	=	1 if start before 0600
		0 if otherwise
E2	=	1 if start before 0630
		0 if otherwise
E3	=	1 if start before 0700
		0 if otherwise
E4	=	1 if start before 0730
		0 if otherwise

Table 6.9
Results of estimations with ORGN data using start time dummies

(standard errors in brackets)

Model	A	B	C
ASC - Air v Car	1.867	1.803	1.793
	(0.116)	(0.117)	(0.117)
ASC - Rail 1 v Car	2.039	1.849	1.826
	(0.072)	(0.086)	(0.089)
ASC - Rail 2 v Car	1.524	1.308	1.304
	(0.059)	(0.081)	(0.081)
Cost (£)	-0.033	-0.034	-0.034
	(0.001)	(0.001)	(0.001)
Time (hours)	-0.399	-0.321	-0.297
	(0.026)	(0.033)	(0.039)
E1		-0.409	-0.340
		(0.106)	(0.121)
E2			-0.131
			(0.105)
Rho-bar-squared	0.4034	0.4041	0.4042
Log-likelihood	-5774.6	-5767.43	-5766.44
Values of time (p/min)	20.00	15.52	14.68
	(1.30)	(1.65)	(1.90)
Values of ASC's (£):			
Air v Car	56.58	53.03	52.74
Rail 1 v Car	61.79	54.38	53.71
Rail 2 v Car	46.18	38.47	38.35
Rail 1 v Rail 2	15.61	15.91	15.35
Values of early starts:			
Before 0600		12.03	13.85
0600-0629			3.85

We did not experiment with dummies for arriving home late because the time at which the traveller arrives at home is a function of the start time and journey time. Although values of the early start time dummies will be related to the length of time spent away from home, we thought there was probably enough variability in the relationship between these 2 variables across the different ranking exercises to avoid serious problems due to multicollinearity.

Use of E1, E2, E3 and E4 is equivalent to attaching different coefficients to time savings at different times in the morning. To calculate the disutility of an additional minute of travel time when this time occurs, say between 0600 and 0629, the estimated coefficient of E2 should be multiplied by 2, added to the estimated time coefficient, and the sum divided by 60.

Table 6.9 shows the initial results for the ORGN data. The Alternative Specific Constants show that car is much disliked for such journeys. Air and first class rail are closely matched. Second class rail was found to be valued between £15 and £16 less than first class for this round trip. With just over 6 hours as the typical round trip journey time, this converts to about 4 pence per minute of in-vehicle time, i.e. these business travellers were willing to pay 4 pence per minute extra to travel first class as against second. The very earliest (E1) of the 'start time' dummies proved significant (model B), with E2 plausible but not significantly different from zero (model C). Using model B gives a £12 penalty for starting before 0600. Including the early start dummy has a big influence on the estimated value of travel time. Without the dummy the value of time is estimated at 20 pence per minute, but with the dummy this falls to 15.5 pence per minute. This is because, in the choices offered, longer travel times (quite naturally) tended to involve early starts.

We then considered whether the cost effect was 'linear'. To do this we defined additional cost dummy variables operating above stated levels of cost. Thresholds at £50 and £75 were significant for the ECML data, while only the threshold at £75 was significant for the ORGN data. These results suggested a non-linear cost effect was at work in the data. This was perhaps to have been expected given the cost differences between modes in the Stated Preference experiment were generally not small (often in excess of £30). Large cost changes will have a non-marginal effect on respondents' incomes and hence their marginal utility of income could be expected to be an increasing function of travel costs. Hensher and Louviere (1983) obtained a quadratic effect for international air travel, where again cost differences between options are large. We therefore added a quadratic cost term to models for the ECML and ORGN data.

In both cases the quadratic cost term was highly significant and the linear cost term loses significance, though only just so in the case of the ORGN data. The quadratic cost model fits the ECML data almost as well as the model with thresholds at £50 and £75. All further modelling on this data set was, therefore, performed assuming a quadratic cost effect. In the case of the ORGN data the model with the £75 threshold performs slightly better than the model with the quadratic cost term. However, because there are good priori reasons for expecting a continuous rather than a discrete non-linear effect, the quadratic formulation seemed more appropriate. Dropping the linear cost term gives a significant loss in the explanatory power of the model and hence, both the linear and quadratic cost terms were retained for further analysis of the ORGN data set. The average values of time from the two models are almost the same: 11.6 pence per minute for the ECML data and 11.8 pence per minute for the ORGN data.

Next we examined the stability of the estimated cost and time parameters across different sample segments. In particular, we were interested in finding out whether these parameters varied according to respondent's incomes and work hours. The utility theory of consumer choice, which underlies our estimated models, suggests the cost coefficient, and hence the marginal utility of income (for a given cost), will decrease as income increases. To test this hypothesis we allowed the cost coefficient to vary across the four income groups: 0 - £10,000 per annum; £10,001 - £15,000 per annum; £15,001 - £20,000 per annum; £20,000+ per annum.

For the ECML data this was done by constructing a different cost variable for each of the four income groups, that is cost variable is partitioned by income (see MVA, ITS, TSU (1987); Judge, Hill, Griffiths, Lutkepohl and Lee (1982)). Allowing this variation in the cost coefficient gives a substantial, statistically significant improvement in model fit. The cost coefficients differ significantly (when comparing adjacent income groups) and decrease (in absolute value) as income increases. Value of time estimates increase by a factor of 2.4 when moving from the bottom to the top income group i.e. range from approximately 8 pence per minute to 19 pence per minute.

For the ORGN data constraints imposed by computing resources meant it was not possible to partition each of the two cost coefficients by the 4 income groups. To get around this problem each of the two cost terms was divided by the median income for the four income groups: £0-10k, £10-15k, £15-20k, >£20k. This is equivalent to imposing the constraint that values of time are linearly related to income. Although this constraint was rejected by the ECML data, we found imposing a linear income constraint on the cost coefficients for the ORGN data gave better results than the alternative solution of imposing the constraint that the relative size of the cost coefficients (i.e. of cost and cost squared) be the same for each of the four income groups. Dividing the cost coefficients by income does give a significant improvement in model fit, once again supporting the hypothesis that values of time are positively related to income. Values of time increase from 8.8 pence per minute, for respondents in the bottom income group, to 25 pence per minute for the top income group.

In addition to the income effect on the cost coefficient, it could also be hypothesised that people with high incomes have less spare time than others, because they spend more time working, in which case the marginal utility of time should be observed to increase with income. A more direct test of this hypothesis could be carried out by allowing the time coefficient to vary by hours worked, rather than by the proxy variable income. Our approach here was to use the sum of time normally spent at work plus time spent commuting each day as an indicator of the severity of an individual's time constraints. This sum we refer to as the length of the work day. Commuting time was added to hours worked as this seemed to give a better indication, than just hours worked, of the amount of 'free' time each individual had available for leisure activities. For some people this will underestimate the amount of work done, because lack of relevant data means our measure does not take account of work done at weekends or differences in holidays. In both samples income and length of work day are, as expected, correlated, with higher incomes being associated with longer work days.

We also had data on whether respondents worked fixed hours, flexitime or variable hours (i.e. until the job was done). Segmenting the time coefficient by these 3 types of work hours gave a poorer explanation of the data than that obtained with the segmentation by length of work day.

The results obtained from segmenting the time coefficient by the length of the work day show, for both data sets, the addition of this segmentation gives a significant improvement in model fit even after allowing for income as discussed earlier. For the ECML sample only people with a work day of more than 10.5 hours have a significantly larger marginal utility of time than the rest of the sample, while for the ORGN sample (Table 6.10) people with work days of less than 9.5 hours, 9.5 to 10.5 hours and over 10.5 hours all have significantly different marginal utilities of time. The results are consistent with the hypothesis that people with longer work days are more time constrained/ have less leisure time than others, and hence have higher marginal utilities of time.

For the ORGN data, we have found that the cost coefficients differ significantly by income and the value of the time coefficient depends on the length of the work day. Combining these two sources of coefficient variation in a single model gives the value of time estimates listed in the last column of Table 6.10. This model fits the data much better than models containing only one of the two sources of coefficient variation.

We can derive rating factors for individuals with different

income/length of work day characteristics. The base sample fraction comprises individuals whose incomes are £10,000 or less and whose work day is less than 9.5 hours. The rating factors one should apply to value of time estimates for this base group are:

	Segment	Factor
Length of work day:	<9.5 hours	1.0
	>9.5 hours	1.5
Income:	£0-15k (median £8.3k)	1.0
	£10-15k (median £11.8k)	1.4
	£15-20k (median £17.1k)	2.1
	>£20k (median £24.3k)	2.9

Comparison with other studies

Behavioural value of time estimates for UK long distance business travellers have been derived by three other studies: University of Leeds (1971); University of Southampton (1971); Steer, Davis and Gleave (SDG) (1981). Wardman (1986) has estimated values of time for short distance (less than 25 miles one way) business travellers. We have converted the estimates from these studies to 1984 values by inflating or deflating by the relevant change in average full-time earnings, as measured by the New Earnings Survey (Department of Employment (1984)) (see Table 6.11).

Comparison of these values shows our results are similar to those obtained by SDG and University of Southampton. Also, most studies find that business travellers value time savings at much higher rates than leisure travellers. The one exception to this is Wardman (op.cit.) who found leisure and business travellers, making urban car journeys across the River Tyne, had approximately the same values of time. The low business values of time obtained in that study may be explained by the alternative use of the time savings. Urban travellers making a short business trip are likely to use travel time savings for work, whereas long distance business travellers are more likely to use travel time savings for leisure purposes, and hence these time savings are of greater value to the individual concerned.

Table 6.10

Value of time estimates allowing cost and time coefficients to vary by income and work hours - ORGN data (p/min)*

(standard errors in brackets)

	Income on cost	Income on time	Length of work day on time	Income on cost, length of work day on time
0-£10k	8.80	3.18		6.79
	(1.22)	(2.13)		(1.33)
£10-15k	12.54	10.43		9.64
	(1.74)	(2.98)		(1.88)
£15-20k	18.11	{		13.92
	(2.52)	{ 17.37		(2.72)
>£20k	25.84	{ (4.19)		19.86
	(3.60	{		(3.88)
Hours > 9.5				
£0-10k				10.26
				(1.31)
£10-15k				14.54
				(1.86)
£15-20k				21.01
				(2.68)
>£20k				29.97
				(3.83)
Hours <9.5			5.11	
			(1.88)	
Hours 9.5-10.5			14.17	
			(1.95)	
Hours 10.5+			17.53	
			(2.1)	
LL(0)	-9314.51	-9314.51	-9314.51	-9314.51
LL(M)	-5447.18	-5462.80	-5469.00	-5438.57
Observations	2212	2212	2212	2212
Rho-bar-sq	0.4150	0.4133	0.4126	0.4159

* All values of time are for time savings after 0530 and are evaluated at the average cost of travel in the stated preference experiment, i.e. £63.25

Table 6.11
Value of time estimates for business travellers
(1984 prices)

Study	Value of time for business travellers	Ratio of business to leisure travellers' value of time (approximate values)
University of Leeds (1971)	30-50% of hourly household income	3 - 5
University of Southampton (1971)	10.5p/min	n.a.
Steer, Davis and Gleave (1981)	9.5p/min	5
Wardman (1986)	4.2p/min	1

This study:
   ECML
   ORGN
	11.6p/min
	11.8p/min
		2 - 3*

*   This estimate was obtained by taking the ratio of the values of time estimated above to those found by Bradley, Marks and Wardman (1986) for long distance car, coach and rail travellers.

Our work has shown that values of time depend on the traveller's income and work hours. Thus, when comparing the value of time estimates given in Table 6.11, one should allow for differences in the composition of the samples for each study. Unfortunately we do not possess sufficient data to do this properly. In the University of Leeds (1971) study the median income of business travellers was approximately 70 per cent more than the median household income for the UK as a whole (Central Statistical Office (1970)). The median personal income of respondents to our surveys exceeded the average level of earnings by a similar amount. The median 'household' income for respondents to Wardman's survey of business travellers was £11.4k. This is considerably below the median 'personal' incomes for our two samples (£14.4k, £13.1k) and probably, in part, explains why value of time estimates derived in Wardman's study are less than half the estimates we have obtained. University of Southampton report only the occupational status of their sample: 52 per cent were managerial and 28 per cent were professional staff. These proportions are very similar to those for our ORGN sample, though not for the ECML sample which contained a much higher fraction of professional staff and a correspondingly smaller fraction of managerial staff. SDG do not report socio-economic data for their sample of business travellers.

SDG used the results of a hypothetical journey planning game to derive their value of time estimates. In this game business travellers (on trains) were asked to rank 9 different train services each of which was described by cost, travel time, frequency and, in some cases, the number of interchanges. Although it is now clear that the business travellers is making the travel decision, it is not clear in SDG's report who is paying for (receiving the benefit of) any (hypothetical) fare increases (decreases). This is important because one might expect the traveller to be more generous with the firm's rather than his/her own money (Marks, 1986b).

From the above evidence all that can be said is that, with the exception of Wardman (1986), our samples appear to be roughly similar, in terms of their socio-economic characteristics, to those collected by the other studies listed in Table 6.11.

6.6 Evidence on business travellers' values of overcrowding and service frequency

This chapter has concentrated on findings regarding business travellers from surveys conducted as part of a project directed solely at business travel. However, business travellers are often encountered by surveys of travellers generally. Clearly, there will be a problem of assessing results regarding business travellers answering a general purpose Stated Preference questionnaire since it will not be clear who is actually paying the monetary cost. Business travellers might therefore be expected to choose the option which is best on all the non-cost attributes. In practice, however, this does not usually happen. Having established, in previous sections, business travellers' values of time, we are in a good position to judge other responses. We report below the results for business travellers encountered in one of the surveys reported in Chapter 5, concerning overcrowding and service frequency.

Table 6.12 shows values for business travellers which are roughly two to three times those of leisure travellers in the same sample. Given the evidence in Table 6.11 this makes the results extremely plausible. Second class business travellers have values roughly two-thirds those of first class business travellers, which

99

again seems eminently plausible, and dispels any worries that respondents were ignoring the costs. With values of time presumably around 14p/minute (in 1987), we see that respondents are not much concerned at having to travel in a full train, but that they are prepared to pay for a frequent service. Therefore improving from an hourly to half-hourly service would reduce average adjustment time from 15 minutes to 7.5 minutes, and this would be valued roughly equivalently to a 5 minute journey time reduction, or £1 in 1987 values.

Table 6.12
Value of crowding and adjustment time
for business travellers (1987 values)

	First Class	Second Class
Travelling in full train (p/min)	3.08	2.18
Standing 30 minutes	£15.21	£12.54
Standing 60 minutes	£23.51	£15.97
Departing earlier than desired (p/min)	13.73	8.14
Departing later than desired (p/min)	14.33	9.96

NB: The crowding variables are taken relative to travelling in a lightly loaded train.

Having to stand is clearly disliked. As with leisure travellers, it appears that there is a fixed penalty of having to stand at all (disrupting plans for relaxing, working, eating, chatting whilst travelling), as well as a penalty per minute of standing. The values indicated are so high that the avoidance of standing for a small number of business travellers would be sufficient to justify adding an extra coach to the train. The values obtained from this survey were, in fact, used by BR to justify the lengthening of trains on that route, the East Coast Main Line, see Ball (1991).

6.7 Conclusion

In this chapter we have considered both what employers are willing to pay for their employees to save time, and what the employees themselves would be willing to pay to save time when on a long distance business trip. The willingness to pay of employers was a little above that given by the standard approach of assuming that

100

they would be willing to pay the equivalent hourly marginal cost of labour (wage plus overheads). For employees the value is somewhat lower, although still greatly in excess of the value of leisure time savings. This is not surprising given the unsocial hours and exhausting nature of many of the journeys studied. In applying these values to forecasting actual behaviour, the problem remains of disentangling the extent to which a change in rail service might lead to a change in company travel policy, and the extent to which individuals are able to claim set travel allowances regardless of the mode they actually use.

7 Commuting

ROGER MACKETT AND CHRIS NASH

7.1 Introduction

Rail commuting takes place into a number of British cities, but whilst in most cases the daily flow consists of a few thousand commuters, in the case of Central London it is over 800,000 (with rather more than half of these being on British Rail services and the remainder on the rail services of London Transport). This chapter will therefore concentrate on the analysis of commuter journeys into London.

All the methods of analysis discussed in previous chapters can be applied to commuters. For instance there have been extensive studies of commuting using time series regression analysis of ticket sales data, whilst Stated and Revealed Preference mode choice models were both used in a study of North Kent commuters undertaken for the Department of Transport. The evidence from some of these studies will be considered in Section 7.3.

However, there are some particular problems involved in analysing the commuting market. Firstly, in the case of London, British Rail has a very dominant position regarding commuting, particularly at the longer distance end of the market (Table 7.1). Although for an individual, there may be a choice of whether to work in Central London or not, as long as the number of jobs in Central London remains constant, these jobs will be filled by commuters travelling in from somewhere. Thus there is likely to be a strong cross-elasticity effect between rail routes, and analysing routes one at a time in isolation from each other is not likely to be adequate.

Table 7.1

Central London commuter trips by mode in the peak period (000's)

| | British Rail | London Transport | | | All Public Transport | Private Car | Motor Cycle/ Pedal Cycle | All Private Transport | All Transport |
		Rail	Bus	Coach					
1961	452	430	209		1089	125	49	174	1264
1966	456	416	175		1047	142	24	166	1213
1971	460	385	146		991	163	12	174	1165
1972	442	381	144		967	172	13	185	1152
1973	435	370	144		949	173	14	188	1137
1974	419	375	143		936	170	13	183	1119
1975	403	344	148		895	162	19	181	1075
1976	401	316	151		868	165	22	187	1055
1977	400	320	139		859	170	22	192	1051
1978	410	325	133	10	878	176	24	200	1078
1979	421	347	112	10	890	173	22	195	1085
1980	412	305	103	10	830	184	27	211	1041
1981	394	336	105	16	851	173	26	199	1050
1982	390	283	99	22	794	197	39	236	1030
1983	384	323	97	24	828	180	33	213	1041
1984	386	350	94	25	855	180	26	206	1061
1985	401	364	94	26	885	171	26	197	1082
1986	421	381	91	25	918	166	21	187	1105
1987	449	401	79	21	950	161	19	180	1130
1988	468	411	80	21	980	160	17	177	1157

Source: Transport Statistics, DTp various years.

Note: The London Transport rail figures exclude passengers transferring from British Rail services. Coach figures include commuting, tourist and Green Line coaches, but not, for example, coaches provided by any employer for its workers.

Secondly, changes in the volume of rail commuting tend to be associated more with changes in the number of jobs in Central London and in the location of the people filling them than with changes in mode split. Thus to be useful a forecasting model must address these locational and land use issues, rather than simply working with transport system variables. More than that, though, one would expect that transport system changes would themselves influence these land-use variables. Rising rail fares, for instance, would tend to raise the demand for housing in Inner London, and to reduce the supply of labour to fill Central London jobs. These effects would in turn tend to raise house prices in Inner London, and wages in Central London. The net effect would be to encourage a redistribution of both employment and population such that rail commuting to Central London is reduced. In other words, we need more than a simple land-use transportation model of the traditional school; we need a model which represents the effects of transport on land-use as well as vice versa. Section 7.2 considers some of the changes in commuting into Central London in more detail.

Section 7.4 of this chapter considers some empirical evidence on the significance of these sorts of effects, based on surveys conducted in the early 1980's. The following two sections examine two approaches to modelling these effects. The first utilises a long established aggregate model - the Leeds Integrated Land-use Transport model (LILT). The second looks at a more experimental disaggregate approach to the problem.

7.2 The residential, employment and transport system in south-east England

Like most western cities, London has been undergoing two processes in recent years: decentralisation and a shift from public to private transport. However, more recently there seem to have been some changes to this picture. Table 7.1 shows the number of peak hour (7 to 10am) arrivals entering Central London (an area approximately surrounded by the Circle Line on the London Underground).

As Table 7.1 shows, from 1961 to early 1980 there was a steady decrease in the numbers entering Central London, associated with a general decline in the numbers travelling by public transport, but an increase in the use of the car (with a temporary decrease in 1975, in the wake of the fuel crisis of 1973-74 which caused a large petrol price increase).

However, since 1981 there have been some interesting changes, partly associated with the public transport fares policy of the Greater London Council. In October 1982, London Transport bus and Underground fares were reduced by 32 per cent and zonal fares introduced on the buses and the central area on the Underground. Both modes, particularly the latter, showed an increase in patronage. In March 1983, following a House of Lords ruling, bus and Underground fares were increased by 96 per cent, leading to a decline in patronage. In May 1983 London Transport reduced fares by an average of 25 per cent, with zonal fares extended to the whole of the Underground, which led to growth on the Underground, but had little effect on the buses, except perhaps a slowing down in the rate of decline. All this time British Rail patronage was declining. However, in January 1985 British Rail introduced the Capitalcard, which permits travel on rail, bus and Underground services, within chosen concentric zones, so that extra journeys could be made at zero marginal cost. In January 1986 this scheme was extended as an 'add-on' to a conventional rail season ticket and in January 1989 merged with the London Transport travelcard. The effect of these recent changes has been to reverse the decline in the demand for rail and Underground travel so that the peak demand is at the level of the mid 1970's and still growing. Travel by car into Central London has shown a corresponding decline since 1982. This all suggests that modal split into Central London is sensitive to the relative cost of travel by the various modes, but that it is not just the mean fare payable that determines the modal share.

Not only has there been a modal shift, but also there has been a growth in the total numbers travelling from the nadir in 1982 back to the level of the mid 1970's. Since the cost of travel by rail, which is the only mode that has increased its share of the market, has not fallen, it is clear that this growth is not due solely to changes in travel costs, and must be due to other factors, such as employment growth.

Some other features of Table 7.1 are noteworthy. The deregulation of long distance coach travel under the 1980 Transport Act was followed by a steady growth in coach commuting to 1984, but this has levelled off. Stage carriage bus services have declined over this whole period, with some temporary increases after the cost of car travel increased in 1975 and in 1981. There is no sign of any stemming of the decline as a result of tendering of bus services in London. In fact, tendering has been concentrated in the suburbs, and is unlikely to have had much impact on Central London as yet.

7.3   Previous studies

Price elasticity

A number of studies have used time series analysis of ticket sales data, taking advantage of the considerable changes in real fares resulting from changing policies, and of service improvements as a result of modernisation. In the case of London Transport, these studies have concentrated on the system as a whole, and have found low price elasticities of the order of 0.2 for rail, those for bus being somewhat higher (Frerk, Lindsey and Fairhurst, 1981). For British Rail, the most extensive published study is that of Oldfield and Tyler (1981), which examined 140 flows of traffic into Central London from stations between 20 and 120km out., using four-weekly ticket sales data for the period 1971 to 1978. For season tickets, a mean price elasticity of around 0.5 was estimated, although with considerable variation seemingly not related to distance. Even this was strictly a short run elasticity, and further unpublished work suggests that when lags are incorporated into the model a substantially higher long run elasticity is obtained. Similarly, Glaister (1983), in a study of two routes which used a hierarchical logit model to examine both the choice of whether to travel and the selection of ticket type, found price elasticities in the range 0.7 to 0.9.

Given that this data relates to individual routes studied in isolation from each other, it is a little difficult to interpret the results. However, as fares tend to move together on all routes (albeit with an element of selectively large increases, for instance where service levels have improved), the most reasonable interpretation seems to be that this is what happens on the route in question when all fares throughout the system rise by an equal proportion. Thus the high elasticity measured does not simply represent a reallocation of demand to routes where fares have not increased.

So what is happening to the people who cease to commute by rail after a fares increase? Some of them may have switched mode, although given the dominance of rail this seems unlikely to explain such high elasticities. Some may have moved homes closer to London, and switched to London Transport, or obtained jobs locally. However, as long as the overall pattern of locations of jobs and homes is unchanged, such moves can only take place as part of a wholesale reallocation of jobs and homes.

Service quality

Evidence from this sort of study on service quality is less clear. Oldfield and Tyler estimated a frequency elasticity of 0.6, but this was based on just one or two flows where high speed trains had been introduced. More evidence is provided by a study of the effects of the electrification of the Great Northern suburban line in Hertfordshire (Hertfordshire County Council, 1980). Both frequency and journey time were improved, the latter by up to 40% at outer suburban stations but less dramatically closer in. This appeared to produce traffic increases of the order of 10-20%, with little change at some inner suburban stations and the greatest growth at particular stations in rapidly developing areas further out. Much of this growth appeared to be at the expense of other rail services (British Rail or London Transport); there was also some evidence of diversion from car and bus. Subsequent electrification of the Midland route through Hertfordshire from Bedford to the City has produced substantially greater traffic increases, although it is unclear how far these would have occurred anyway. The importance of quality of service to commuters is borne out by subsequent market research and Stated Preference studies.

Mode choice

Many studies have been made of the mode choice decisions of Central London commuters over the years. It is well established that car is often used by people who either need their car in the course of work, or who have facilities for use of the car provided by their employer, ranging from a free parking space up to a free car and petrol (GLC, 1984). The recent, if limited, growth in coach commuting has presented another option which formed the subject of a major study undertaken as part of a Department of Transport project on the value of travel time savings. This was a study of commuters into London from North Kent undertaken in July, 1983.

Contact was made with rail and coach users in the Gravesend - Medway - Sittingbourne area of Kent by means of a mail back questionnaire. This was used to screen out non-commuters and those who would not consider the mode not being used as a possible alternative to their current mode (to this extent the survey is biased towards the less captive users of both modes). A follow up questionnaire was then sent out, to which 1,381 usable replies were received. Relative characteristics of rail and coach commuters are summarised in Table 7.2.

Generally the attractiveness of commuter coach services is believed to be that they offer slower but cheaper means of travel. Thus it is expected that they would be utilised by poorer and mainly younger commuters than those who chose rail. To some extent, this appears to be the case; 37% of coach users are under 25 and 41% are female, compared with 21% and 30% respectively for rail. The mean income of coach users appeared to be around £8400, compared with £11000 for rail. Nevertheless over 50% of coach users were males over the age of 25.

Table 7.2

Table 7.2
Characteristics of North Kent rail and coach commuters

(column %)

	Rail Users	Coach Users
Age		
Under 25	20.5	36.8
25-44	54.1	44.7
45-64	25.3	17.9
Over 65	0.1	0.0
Missing	0.0	0.7
Sex		
Male	70.2	58.9
Female	29.8	40.7
Missing	0.0	0.3
Income (£ pa)		
Under 5000	4.9	9.6
5000-7000	16.5	31.6
7000-9000	18.9	20.3
9000-11000	20.8	17.0
11000-13000	11.6	10.1
13000-15000	9.3	4.3
15000-20000	12.1	2.8
Over 20000	5.8	1.0
Missing	0.1	3.3

Source: 1983 North Kent Survey

Table 7.3 compares the total journey times for the two modes. Although rail is substantially faster for the in-vehicle part of the journey, part but not all of this is compensated for by the better door-to-door penetration of the coach services. Around a third of all coach users claimed a faster door-to-door time by coach than rail. Whilst there may be an element of self-justification in these replies, it does seem likely that there is a section of the population for which coach is very competitive on journey time, perhaps because some new housing estates are located closer to the motorway than to the railway.

Table 7.4 shows that coach does indeed possess a considerable price advantage over rail, particularly when the reduced need to use feeder modes is taken into account. Table 7.5 shows some evidence on the perceived quality of service of the two modes by both rail and coach users. Not surprisingly, coach users tended to believe the quality of service offered by coach was better, whilst rail users considered the reverse to be true. However, considerable numbers of rail users thought coach the superior mode in terms of ability to get a seat, seating comfort and pleasantness of the environment. There was also evidence that cancellation of coach services was less of a problem than for rail.

Table 7.3
Difference in total travel time compared
with alternative mode

(column %)

	Rail Users	Coach Users
Alternative over 40 minutes slower	35.8	4.1
Alternative 31-40 minutes slower	18.2	1.9
Alternative 21-30 minutes slower	19.7	6.2
Alternative 11-20 minutes slower	13.1	7.2
Alternative 1-10 minutes slower	5.8	11.9
Alternative 0-9 minutes quicker	3.0	20.8
Alternative 10-19 minutes quicker	2.1	21.0
Alternative 20-29 minutes quicker	1.1	13.2
Alternative 30-39 minutes quicker	0.1	7.6
Alternative over 40 minutes quicker	1.1	6.2

Source: 1983 North Kent survey

Table 7.4
Mean return journey cost (£)

	Rail Users		Coach Users	
	Rail	Coach Alternative	Coach	Rail Alternative
Main Mode Cost	3.579	2.418	2.442	4.172
Feeder Mode Cost (Home End)	0.270	0.060	0.009	0.498
Parking Cost	0.225	0.185	0.109	0.299
Feeder Mode Cost (Work End)	0.183	0.010	0.001	0.071
TOTAL	4.257	2.673	2.561	5.240

Source: 1983 North Kent Survey

Table 7.5
Perceived quality of service of rail and coach

(row %)

	Train better than coach	About the same	Coach better than train	Missing
Certainty of getting a seat				
Coach Users	1.6	15.8	82.3	0.3
BR Users	22.5	45.2	31.7	0.6
Ease of reading				
Coach Users	20.1	38.7	40.6	0.7
BR Users	52.4	35.9	11.0	0.6
Ease of resting				
Coach Users	9.6	29.6	60.7	0.2
BR Users	45.3	38.3	15.9	0.5
Seating comfort				
Coach Users	11.3	19.2	69.2	0.2
BR Users	29.0	30.4	39.9	0.6
Pleasant environment				
Coach Users	4.8	12.2	82.8	0.2
BR Users	35.8	34.2	28.8	1.3

Source: 1983 North Kent Survey

Overall, then, the picture of coach as a cheaper but poorer quality mode is borne out by this study. But coach does have some quality of service advantages in this corridor, which it must be said was at the time one of the least attractive services of British Rail, with elderly rolling stock and chronic overcrowding. It is also the corridor in which coach services have made by far their greatest inroads into the rail market, although even here rail remains the dominant mode.

The data collected in the study was used to model the choices, using both a logit model on the Revealed Preferences, and a linear logit model to study the response to a Stated Preference questionnaire. Given the large sample and clearcut tradeoffs of time against cost, this represented a near-ideal situation in which to estimate Revealed Preference models, and the two approaches gave fairly similar results. Values of time estimated were relatively high (of the order of 3p per minute), but varied in the expected way across the sample according to age and income (Wardman, 1988).

7.4   Survey evidence

The above suggests that the elasticity of demand for rail commuting to Central London is quite high, and that only part of this can be explained by switches in mode.   We must therefore examine changes in location of home or job as a possible explanation of this elasticity.

In this section, we consider the results of surveys undertaken of London commuters as part of an ESRC funded study in 1981.   The aim of the surveys was partly to discover characteristics of existing commuters, but more importantly to explore their behaviour over time; when they had changed home, job or mode of travel and why. Two surveys were conducted on a self completion basis - one of workers at eight major employers in Central London (two banks, a building society, an insurance company, a public transport operator, a public utility and a government department).   This is subsequently referred to as the 'organisations' questionnaire.   In total some 6,000 questionnaires were distributed, yielding 2,321 usable replies.   The second source was the season ticket records of six railway stations in Hertfordshire (Hitchin, Welwyn Garden City, Potters Bar, Bishops, Stortford, Broxbourne and Theobalds Grove), and is referred to as the Hertfordshire survey.   These stations were chosen to give a spread of distances from Central London ranging from 15 to 50 kilometres, on two lines, one of which had remained virtually unchanged since electrification in the mid 1960's, whilst the other had recently received substantial improvements as a result of electrification completed in 1978.   On our behalf, British Rail distributed questionnaires to a sample of existing and past season ticket holders.   Nearly 3,000 questionnaires were distributed, yielding 1,837 usable replies.   In both cases follow-up interviews were held with a sample of some 150-200 of those originally surveyed.

In both surveys, more than half those responding had occupations which could broadly be called 'Managerial and Professional', with nearly all the remainder being secretarial or clerical.   There is of course a major contrast between the two groups (Table 7.6).   The former are predominantly male, married and over 21.   Secretarial and clerical staff are mainly female, young and with a substantial proportion (nearly half) living with their parents.   It seems reasonable to suppose that the travel response

111

of the two groups to changes in fares and service levels would be very different.

Table 7.6
Characteristics of rail commuters

(column %, with absolute numbers)

| | --------Hertfordshire-------- | | ------Central London------ | |
	Professional /Managerial	Secretarial /Clerical	Professional /Managerial	Secretarial /Clerical
Sex				
Male	82.7	20.5	85.2	33.2
Female	17.3	79.5	14.81	66.8
Age				
16-21	3.9	42.7	5.3	42.1
22-35	44.8	36.8	45.1	35.1
36-45	23.1	6.6	18.6	5.9
46-70	28.1	13.9	31.0	16.8
Life cycle				
(1) Single person household	6.1	7.2	14.3	8.6
(2) Couple	27.4	28.6	26.2	26.1
(3) Couple with children	9.1	43.2	8.2	42.7
(4) Living with parents	53.8	15.9	46.3	18.3
(5) Other*	3.6	5.1	5.1	4.4
Cars				
0	6.1	12.6	14.3	21.4
1	59.6	53.0	61.5	51.1
2+	34.2	34.5	24.1	27.6

* Mainly living with friends

Source: Hertfordshire and Organisations survey

A further interesting result to emerge was the high degree of home and job mobility of the sample as a whole. In the Hertfordshire sample, it emerged that nearly a third of those surveyed had changed either job, or home or both within the last year. Of course, this proportion was higher in the younger age groups, which included school leavers taking up their first job, people leaving their parents home on marriage and so on.

Nevertheless, although there were substantial numbers of managers who had experienced exactly the same journey to work for more than 10 years, the overall picture is one of a surprisingly dynamic market.

Table 7.7
Present workplace location and mode
of lapsed season-ticket holders

(% of total in brackets)

| | ----------Present Workplace---------- | | | |
Main Mode	Central London	Rest of GLC	Else-where	TOTAL
Rail from same station*	37	13	7	57
	(14.9)	(5.2)	(2.8)	(22.9)
Rail from another station	9	0	1	10
	(3.6)	(0.0)	(0.4)	(4.0)
Not rail	20	37	103	160
	(8.0)	(14.9)	(41.4)	(64.3)
TOTAL	66	50	111	227
	(26.5)	(20.1)	(44.6)	(91.2)
Of which non-rail:				
Car driver, car	14	32	78	124
passenger & motorcycle	(5.6)	(12.9)	(31.3)	(49.8)
Bus	0	2	5	7
	(0.0)	(0.8)	(2.0)	(2.8)
Underground	4	2	0	6
	(1.6)	(0.8)	(0.0)	(2.4)
Other	2	1	17	20
	(0.8)	(0.4)	(6.8)	(8.0)

* Note: 'Same station' is defined as the station at which their season ticket record is kept. A further 22 respondents were unemployed.

Source: Hertfordshire Survey

One aspect of the Hertfordshire survey was that it covered a total of 249 former holders of rail season tickets to Central London who had failed to renew their season tickets. Of this number, a small proportion were still commuting to Central London by rail, either from a different station or using a different type of ticket. Some were commuting to Central London by alternative modes, usually private ones. But by far the majority had changed work location, usually combining this with a switch to private transport. A further 22 respondents were no longer in employment. It thus appears that ceasing to work in Central London is by far the dominant reason for ceasing to commute by rail (Table 7.7).

The interviews provided more evidence on this issue. Very few people gave transport reasons for actually changing home or job. Job changes were mainly linked to career progression, whilst home changes were to do with the life cycle effect (with a typical progression from parents' home to small central flat to inner London house or flat to suburban house as people leave home, marry and have children). What did seem obvious, however, was that in choosing a home, or to a lesser extent a job, transport considerations were important. The overall pattern of journeys to work could thus adjust quite rapidly to a change in transport supply, not because particular individuals chose to relocate but because new people coming into the market would locate differently from their predecessors.

It therefore appears that in explaining reactions to transport system changes by commuters, relocation is a key factor. However, as commented earlier, people can only change homes or jobs if alternative ones are available. Thus if someone decides to work locally instead of commuting, then either someone else (perhaps a new entrant into the job market) begins to commute, or else the number of jobs in Central London must decline. At the same time, either a new job must have been created locally or an existing job must have become vacant. These sorts of interactions are of crucial importance when forecasting in aggregate, and it is to these that we turn in the next section.

7.5   The LILT aggregate model

The model

This model is a simplified version of the Leeds Integrated Land-use Transport model (LILT) (Mackett, 1983, 1984). The major simplification is that housing and jobs are specified exogenously in this version. This means that the model is determining the way in which people are allocated to combinations of homes, jobs and modes of transport to work, as a function of the spatial distributions of homes and jobs and the generalised cost of travel to work by the available modes. The model is also disaggregated by social group and car availability.

The model is aggregate. This means that it represents groups of people, rather than individuals. The groupings may be zones, social group, mode of transport and so on. In many cases more than one grouping may be considered simultaneously. If there are large numbers of items in some of the groupings, for example zones, the number of combinations can become huge, since the numbers of combined groupings are multiplied together. It is necessary to consider some of the groupings simultaneously because they cannot be treated as independent. For example, the choice of residential location is a function of workplace location, the generalised cost of travel by the appropriate mode, social status, the availability or otherwise of a car, and the area of previous residence. Given that, in this application of the model, there are 156 zones, there are a very large number of possible combinations. In fact, a very large number of them contain zero people; that is, nobody chooses those particular combinations, since, for example, nobody walks to work from one side of the study are to the other. While it is not relevant to consider the results at the most disaggregated level, by working at that level it is possible to aggregate to various interesting combinations, such as the residential location patterns of rail users.

The model works over time. Typically, a forecast is made twenty years beyond the base year, in four five-year periods. A base or 'most-likely future' forecast is made, and then a policy option is examined by representing the policy in terms of the model inputs, re-running the model, and then comparing the results from the two runs of the models, interpreting the differences as being a result of the policy under consideration.

In the model, it is not assumed that everybody considers changing home and job in each time period. The concept of 'survival' is introduced to represent those who retain the same home or job or both. It is not necessarily assumed that all dwellings and jobs are filled. It is possible to have vacancies. This is useful as vacancies can be regarded as an indication of which areas are unattractive. It is also possible to examine which homes and jobs are chosen first, which is an indicator of attractiveness, taking into account accessibility. A capacity constraint mechanism is used to ensure that demand for homes or jobs does not exceed demand, with the excess being forced to locate elsewhere. The model has been applied previously to Hertfordshire (Mackett, 1985). That paper contains a description of the form of the modelling used in this work.

Method of application

The model has been applied over the period 1982 to 2001 in four intervals of five years each. The periods are usually referred to by the final year for convenience. Thus 1996 refers to change over the period from 1992 to 1996 inclusive. The major objective of the work is to examine the impact of policy options or tests, particularly on rail patronage. The results are compared with a forecast called the 'base run' which is based on the simplest set of assumptions, and incorporates as much known information as possible. For example, the changes in housing and jobs taken from the various structure plans, and the known changes in real transport costs from 1981 to the present have been incorporated. Other than the specific changes discussed previously, transport costs are assumed to be constant in real terms over the forecast period. The tests are carried out by modifying the data in an appropriate form to represent the change as required, for example, changing the rail fares or rail travel times, or introducing extra employment in certain zones. The differences between the base run results and those for a test are interpreted as being due to the change in the inputs. Two important points must be stressed. Firstly, the base run should not be regarded as a forecast of what will happen if none of the changes implied in the tests occur. To carry out a 'pure' forecast would require very detailed analysis of the processes in South-East England. It is assumed that any inadequacies in the forecast over time will not have a significant effect on the differences between the test results and the base run. The second point to be stressed is that it is being assumed that the items being considered in the tests do not have an effect on the exogenous inputs of the distribution of dwellings and jobs. There will be differences in who occupies the dwellings and jobs. The assumption of fixed homes and jobs has been made for two reasons. Firstly it makes the interpretation less complex simply because there are fewer degrees of response, and secondly, the effects of transport cost and service changes on the actions of property developers and employers are not understood sufficiently well to be modelled satisfactorily within this type of framework.

As mentioned above, the analysis will focus on the effects of the tests on rail patronage, in particular where those transferring to or from rail, go to or come from. Such transfers may involve not only switching mode but also changes of home and job, and since the numbers of homes and jobs in each area is finite, there will be consequential impacts on others. This means that the analysis tends to be rather complex, since it is in terms of modes used, residential location, employment locations and the links between them. The results will be in terms of the numbers travelling to work on each mode, both overall and to specific destinations, particularly Central London, the transfer between modes, the numbers travelling along various corridors to London, the numbers of Central London workers choosing to live in various areas, and the differences between those changing home or job and those not doing so. Various indicators of the effects of such responses are calculated including the change in the level of rail revenue and elasticities. It should be stressed that only work trips are being included in this analysis.

General trends

As discussed previously, the tests have been made by comparison with the 'base run'. While this base run has been produced for the purpose of comparison, it is pertinent to make some comments on the way the model behaves in this run since it underlies much of the subsequent analysis.

The results suggest that the overall level of rail patronage is dependent not only on the level of employment in Central London, but also on the rate of change relative to the growth of housing. Rail trips into Central London are currently growing as employment grows, despite the growth in car ownership. This growth is greater than the expansion in available housing in the areas occupied by existing workers in London so there is a physical expansion in the residential areas occupied by Central London workers. In general, the further out such workers live, the greater the probability that they will commute by rail. Once the pressure is reduced by the slowing down in employment growth in Central London, new entrants to the market are on average able to satisfy their housing needs further in. This means that not only does rail patronage decline, but the average distance travelled also declines, so that revenue declines even further. The model is able to help to explain an apparent paradox. It is generally accepted that people tend to move further from the centre of the city as they move through the life-cycle. The results for the base run show that this phenomenon can occur at the individual level simultaneously with a net aggregate inward movement of the residential location of those working in the city centre. This apparent paradox of simultaneous inward and outward movement is explained by the high level of turnover in the residential sector in South-East England whereby new people are entering the market and making different decisions to those that they replace. As employment in Central London slows

117

down there are fewer people seeking homes, so that residential aspirations can be met further in, on average, thus reducing the overall distance from the centre. With time, these people will tend to move outwards, but not as far out as their predecessors. Meanwhile the new entrants will satisfy their housing needs further in. There will be small, compensating, adjustments by other people who do not commute to Central London.

If this analysis is valid, it has serious implications in terms of rail patronage because it means that relatively small changes in the residential and employment patterns at an aggregate level can mask large changes in the spatial linkages at the individual level, and it is the sum of the individual linkages that represents the demand for rail and other modes.

An important feature of this model is that it represents locational changes. When a change in generalised cost is made different spatial allocations are produced. The new allocations are made on the basis of the set of costs representing the available modes. When one mode, for example, rail, is made more attractive some people tend to locate deliberately so that they can use it. This has consequent implications for others because of the finite set of homes and jobs. Whatever the change in the cost for one mode, the locational shifts tend to reinforce the expected direction of change, reflecting the observable attraction towards an area of improved access and the less easily observed lowering of attraction of an area of reduced accessibility. To ignore this locational component of the response means that a significant part of the patronage change is being ignored, plus a large number of changes of trip length with their consequent implications for revenue. The size of the error caused by ignoring the locational effect is a direct function of the size of the cost or other change being studied. Furthermore, in a period of rail fare increase, to ignore the locational effects would underestimate the loss of rail patronage.

The effects of improvements in the quality of the rail service

The improvements in the quality of the rail service have all been represented in terms of a reduction in journey time by rail. Three of the tests come into this category: improvements to the Chiltern and South-East corridors and overall service improvements.

The two corridor improvements show similar effects for a 10 per cent reduction in journey times. There are differences resulting from the nature of the corridors. The Chiltern line is relatively little used for travel to Central London, and so there is scope for a large percentage growth in the rail patronage (about 15 per cent) compared with the South-East sector (about 6 per cent). However, the number of trips involved is much greater in the latter case (growth of about 6000 compared with about 1700). In each case the net growth would continue, at a lower rate, in subsequent years. The growth on the two lines is partly caused by people choosing to live in these areas rather than elsewhere, and so is affected by the availability of dwellings, and indirectly by the availability of local jobs. A large increase in the number of dwellings means that there are more residential opportunities available, while growth in local jobs means that workers will be attracted, possibly by rail. Growth in local commuting occurs when the number of jobs in a zone goes up relative to the number of employed residents. If this occurs during a period of improvement in the rail service, then there is a large growth in local rail commuting. Table 7.8 shows the origins of those transferring to rail as a result of the Chiltern line improvement.

Table 7.8
The origins of those transferring to rail as a
result of the Chiltern Line improvement

| | All trips | | Trips to Central London | |
	Number	%	Number	%
Total growth in rail travellers	2382	100.0	1670	100.0
Number switching from making other rail journeys	662	27.8	1197	71.7
Number making a switch of mode and location	1527	64.2	405	24.3
Number switching mode only	191	8.0	67	4.0

The differences in the transfers to rail in the two improved corridors produce rather different journey time elasticity values (see Tables 7.9 and 7.10). The direct rail values for the period of the increase are -1.11 for the Chiltern line and -0.58 for the South-East sector. These increase to -1.21 and -0.68 respectively over the following ten years. The equivalent values for trips to Central London are -1.29 and -0.50 for the two corridors in the shorter run, and -1.47 and -0.62 respectively ten years after the improvement. The values are larger for trips to Central London than the overall values on the Chiltern line because of the large growth in the numbers travelling to Central London relative to the low base. In the South-East sector rail has less scope for attracting people to travel to Central London in terms of percentage growth because so many already do so from this area.

Table 7.9
Travel time elasticities for rail and cross-elasticities
for other modes for trips from zones on the Chiltern Line
for 1991 and 2001 calculated from changing travel
times on that line

| | All trips from zones on the Chiltern Line | | Trips to Central London on the Chiltern Line | |
	1991	2001	1991	2001
Rail	−1.11	−1.21	−1.29	−1.47
Car	0.07	0.06	0.37	0.18
Bus	0.12	0.11	0.42	0.25
Walk	0.05	0.05	−	−
TOTAL	0.00	0.00	−0.98	−1.13

Note: These elasticities are based on the change along the corridor, and ignore any changes elsewhere in the study area.

Table 7.10
Travel time elasticities for rail and cross-elasticities for other
modes for trips from zones in the south east sector,
for 1991 and 2001, calculated from changing the
travel times in that sector

| | All trips from zones in the South-East sector | | Trips to Central London from the South-East sector | |
	1991	2001	1991	2001
Rail	−0.58	−0.68	−0.50	−0.62
Car	0.10	0.10	0.24	0.20
Bus	0.14	0.14	0.21	0.19
Walk	0.07	0.09	0.11	0.12
TOTAL	−0.00	−0.01	−0.26	−0.34

Note: These elasticities are based on the change along the corridor, and ignore any changes elsewhere in the study area

The cross-elasticities for all journeys are largest for bus, being between 0.10 and 0.15. For trips to Central London the values in the South-East sector are highest for car (0.24 declining over time to 0.20), while on the Chiltern line they are higher for bus (0.42 declining to 0.25).

However, perhaps one of the most important conclusions from this work is that such elasticity values are misleading because they ignore the compensating changes elsewhere. As mentioned above, some of the apparent gain in rail patronage is due to people locating so that they can take advantage of the improved accessibility. In order to show the implications for the elasticity values, indices have been calculated using the net intermodal changes for the whole study area (Table 7.11). These indices have values that are smaller in magnitude, as would be expected because they exclude the net transfer between corridors. The values obtained were -0.81 increasing over time to -0.91 for the Chiltern corridor and -0.43 rising to -0.52 for the South-East sector. The values of the indices for the other modes are all slightly smaller than the equivalent cross-elasticities, as would be expected. From this it seems that to use elasticity values to estimate the growth in rail patronage along a rail corridor in isolation would lead to an overestimate of the overall growth in rail patronage of up to 50 per cent by ignoring the compensating effects elsewhere in the study area.

Table 7.11

Indices of the overall change in modal share in the whole study area relative to the number of trips origins in the Chiltern and South-East corridors

| | Chiltern corridor | | South-East corridor | |
	1991	2001	1991	2001
Rail	−0.81	−0.91	−0.43	−0.52
Car	0.04	0.04	0.08	0.08
Bus	0.12	0.12	0.13	0.14
Walk	0.04	0.04	0.04	0.08
TOTAL	0.00	0.00	0.00	0.00

The calculation of elasticity values for the overall service improvement has no such problem and produces elasticity values of -0.63 increasing over time to -0.69, with an equivalent value for rail trips to Central London of -0.34 to -0.38 (Table 7.12). The values for Central London are lower than the overall values because so many people already commute there by rail, so there is less scope for expansion of this market. These values are smaller than the ones for the Chiltern line, as would be expected, because of the locational effect. They are higher than the values for the South-East sector, which might seem rather curious since that includes the locational shifts from other corridors. However, if the values of the indices of the overall changes are examined it may be noticed that the elasticity values for the overall service improvement lie at about the mid-points of the values for the two corridors. Given the very different natures of the corridors in terms of levels of rail share of the market and strength of connection to Central London, it could be argued that the overall value represents some form of mean of the values for the various corridors, and these two corridors are probably towards the edges of the range.

Table 7.12

Travel time elasticities for rail and cross-elasticities for other modes for 1991 to 2001, calculated from the overall service improvement

| | All trips | | | Trips to Central London | | |
	1991	1996	2001	1991	1996	2001
Rail	-0.63	-0.66	-0.69	-0.34	-0.36	-0.38
Car	0.10	0.11	0.11	0.95	0.97	0.96
Bus	0.21	0.21	0.21	0.91	0.94	0.94
Walk	0.07	0.08	0.08	0.60	0.67	0.68
TOTAL	0.00	0.00	0.00	0.00	0.00	0.00

Note: The travel times were reduced by 10 per cent, except in Central London. Many rail journeys would include a part within Central London, so the actual average reduction is slightly less than 10 per cent, so these values are underestimated.

The cross-elasticities are highest for bus at about 0.21, followed by car at about 0.10 and walk at about 0.07. The cross-elasticity values for trips to Central London are high because the corridors switching effect does not apply, so that the response in terms of losses from other modes is greater.

As well as rail patronage elasticities, rail revenue elasticities have been calculated, and these are higher than the patronage ones because people are relocating and choosing to make longer trips. The values increase with time from -0.86 to -1.00, with rather lower values for trips to Central London increasing over time from -0.46 to -0.56. The values for trips to destinations outside Central London would be very high because the overall values are, in effect, means of the values to Central London and to elsewhere. This suggests that there is considerable potential for revenue generation for trips to various destinations in the South-East as a result of rail service improvement.

To sum up, the results from the model suggest a travel time elasticity value of about -0.63, which increases with time (since the improvement) to about -0.7. Improvements to parts of the rail network would produce equivalent net increases in rail patronage. The current level of rail usage, and changes in the local housing and job markets, would affect the specific values, which can range from about -0.8 for a corridor like the Chiltern line to about -0.4 for an area such as the South-East sector with its high level of rail patronage, ignoring the relocational effects. However, these values are only about three quarters of the elasticity values that are found by calculating the change in patronage on the actual corridor, because some of the apparent growth would be accounted for by people who would have travelled by rail anyway, but have chosen to locate in order to take advantage of the improved access. Not only would the service improvements increase patronage, trips would tend to be longer, so the revenue elasticities are higher, with values of about -0.9, growing over time to about -1.0.

The effects of rail fare changes

The model has been used to examine the effects of a test that involves rail fares: an increase of 1.5 per cent per annum in real terms for fifteen years. The patronage elasticity values are -0.31. This increases over time to -0.35. The value for trips to Central London are lower, at -0.15 increasing over time to -0.19 (see Table 7.13).

The cross-elasticities for the other modes for the fare increase are about 0.05 for car, 0.10 for bus and 0.03 for walk. Larger values are obtained for trips to Central London, with values of about 0.40 for car, 0.36 for bus and 0.25 for walk. All these values, particularly for trips to Central London, tend to increase over time.

The importance of the locational effect in these elasticities is illustrated by Table 7.14. The number of people keeping the same home and job but travelling by another mode is very small. The vast majority of those who switch mode do so in the context of a change of home, or job (or both). Revenue elasticities have been calculated, producing values of about 0.55, which reduce over time with the increasing fares (Table 7.15).

Table 7.13

Fare elasticities for rail and cross-elasticities for other modes for 1991 to 2001, calculated from the 1.5% per annum fare increase test

	All trips			Trips to Central London		
	1991	1996	2001	1991	1996	2001
Rail	-0.31	-0.32	-0.35	-0.15	-0.17	-0.19
Car	0.05	0.05	0.05	0.40	0.42	0.43
Bus	0.09	0.09	0.09	0.36	0.36	0.39
Walk	0.03	0.03	0.03	0.23	0.25	0.27
TOTAL	0.00	0.00	0.00	0.00	0.00	0.00

Table 7.14

Effects of rail fare increase of 1.5% per annum on those who would have travelled by rail in the base run, 1991

	Number	%
Total travelling by rail in the base run	1147889	100.0
Number keeping same home and job, and still travelling by rail	198645	17.3
Number keeping same home and job, but travelling by another mode	3732	0.3
Number changing home or job or both, but still travelling by rail	923420	80.4
Number changing home or job or both, and travelling by another mode	22092	1.9

Table 7.15
Revenue elasticities for rail for 1991 to 2001
calculated from the 1.5% fare increase

	1991	1996	2001
All trips	0.57	0.54	0.49
To Central London	0.76	0.74	0.70

7.6   MASTER model (micro-analytical simulation of transport, employment and residence)

The MASTER model simulates the decision processes that a set of individuals and their households go through over time (Mackett 1988, 1990). It was originally developed as a result of the realisation that a model like LILT could not satisfactorily represent the complexity of response to changes in the transport system.

The model uses 'micro-analytical simulation' (or micro-simulation) in which the progress of a set of individuals and their households through a series of processes is represented. The relationship between the various outcomes of each process and the characteristics of each relevant member of the population is defined by a set of rules or by means of Monte Carlo simulation. Supply-side constraints are incorporated into MASTER model by distinguishing between the decision to enter a decision process, and the satisfactory outcome of the process. If there are no suitable opportunities available the individual remains in the original state.

There are five submodels: demographic, life-cycle and economic activity, employment location, residential location, and transport. The first is to create households. The second establishes those who wish to enter or leave the labour market. In the employment location sub-model a potential new area of work is determined as a function of the cost of travel from the area of residence, so that the cost of travel affects the choice of zone of work.

In the residential location submodel the constraints on the choice of new homes are determined; the total amount of money available for potential owner-occupiers and eligibility, in terms of the local authority's rules for potential council tenants. The distance that a household moves is determined as a function of the tenures of the current and desired dwellings. A potential zone of residence is established using Monte Carlo simulation with the choice of zone a function of the weighted sum of the generalised cost of travel to work by the various modes for the head of the household, so that changes in the cost of travel influence the choice of zone of residence.

The transport processes considered are: becoming a car licence holder; car ownership; car availability; and the choice of mode of transport to work. Becoming a holder of car driving licence is a function of age and sex. Changes in household car ownership are a function of changes in household income, the number of potential car users, and the cost of travel by car and public transport.

Car availability within a household is determined on the basis of rules about order of priority. Modal choice is based on the relative cost of travel by the available modes, with the probabilities of selecting each based on a logit form using generalised cost. A change of mode is only considered when a significant event such as a change of home, the purchase of a car or a large change in travel costs occurs.

The model is still under development, and has been applied to the city of Leeds. However, the model has been used to look into the long term response to changes in the cost of travel and has been compared with the LILT model (Mackett, 1989). It was found that when the changes in location and car ownership are taken into account, elasticity values tend to be higher than the short-term values calculated in other work. Public transport elasticities were found to have greater magnitudes for males compared with females and for those with a car available compared to those without.

7.7 Conclusion

Commuting journeys present particular difficulties where modelling rail demand. Although orthodox elasticity and mode choice models have been applied to commuting, these generally ignore the fact that, in the absence of a change in the overall number of homes and jobs in each location, changes in rail commuting in one corridor will be partly offset by changes in other corridors. Empirical evidence confirms that there is a high level of home and job mobility, and that transport system characteristics affect the choice of home and job of those relocating.

Two approaches to modelling these effects are presented - one aggregate and one disaggregate. Both confirm that simple models give misleading results by ignoring the relocation effect. On the one hand, a model which looks only at the short term effect on mode choice, will substantially understate the true elasticity by ignoring the relocation effect. On the other hand a model which fails to look at consequent changes in other corridors will substantially overstate the effect on rail patronage by ignoring offsetting changes elsewhere.

8   New stations and services

JOHN PRESTON

8.1   Introduction

Passenger rail services in Britain are currently undergoing something of a revival. Since 1970 around 200 new stations have been opened on publicly owned railways in Britain, whilst British Rail (BR) have developed a number of new services. For such new stations and services a problem immediately becomes apparent in that BR's usual approach to demand forecasting is not suitable for predicting the effects of non-marginal changes in levels of service at a local level. This is discussed in section 8.2. As a result, the Institute for Transport Studies has been working since 1982 on the development of suitable forecasting approaches. In the course of this work a variety of forecasting approaches have been developed and tested. These include a simple Trip Rate Model (TRM), a direct demand model that we have entitled an Aggregate Simultaneous Model (ASM) and a disaggregate Mode Choice Model (MCM). These models are all based on some form of Revealed Preference (RP) data and are discussed in section 8.3. An alternative approach has been developed based on asking people directly how often they would use a new facility. This is termed the Stated Intentions (SI) approach. It is well known that such an approach, if applied without adjustment, is likely to lead to overestimates of usage. As a result, a Stated Preference (SP) approach has been devised in order to correct for this bias, as discussed in section 8.4.

The TRM, ASM and MCM models have been compared with actual usage at six new stations in West Yorkshire, as discussed in section 8.5. Unfortunately, the SI/SP approach has not yet (with one partial exception) been applied to a situation where the new facility has subsequently been opened. However, in the study for Leicestershire County Council it was possible to compare the SI/SP forecasts with those produced from a TRM and the ASM. These results are discussed in section 8.6.

In conclusion, it is found that there is a trade-off between the cost/complexity of models and their accuracy. It is felt that models need to be tailored to particular situations and that major investments require more complex approaches. It is shown that the current approaches may be accurate in specific instances but may lack transferability and, hence, further work is required.

This chapter is based on work that was initially undertaken as a Collaborative Award in Science and Engineering research studentship, funded by the Science and Engineering Research Council and BR (Preston, 1987). Subsequent work has included major research contracts for Leicestershire (Preston and Wardman, 1988) and Nottinghamshire (Preston, 1989) County Councils. The work is now continuing with funding from the Economic and Social Research Council. This chapter draws heavily on an earlier article by the author Preston (1991).

Rail re-openings in Britain

Table 8.1 illustrates one aspect of what several commentators have referred to as the rail boom. Up to the mid 1970s the BR passenger rail network was shrinking as the Beeching rationalisation plans were implemented. However, the 1974 Railway Act marked an important watershed and subsequently the network has grown. This is reflected by the number of stations on the BR network which decreased from over 5,000 in 1958 to a low of 2,358 in January 1978. However, since the mid 70s the number of stations opening has begun to exceed the number of closures so that by January 1989 it is estimated that the number of passenger stations exceeds 2,440 (RDS, 1988). Since 1970 almost 200 new stations have been opened on publicly owned passenger rail services in Britain (including Docklands Light Rail and Tyne and Wear Metro).

129

Table 8.1

Opening/closure of stations on publicly owned passenger railways in Britain (includes Tyne and Wear Metro and Docklands Light Rail)

	Opened	Closed	Net balance
1970-74	18	130	-112
1975-79	38	13	+25
1980-84	44	10	+34
1985-88	95	7	+88
TOTAL	195	160	+35

The stations that have been opened may be classified into a number of groups. This chapter concentrates on unmanned halts serving residential areas on existing services, although the SI/SP approach has been used to study stations on completely new services and to consider destinations as well as origins. The work has not considered stations related to light rail systems, InterCity stations, Parkway stations, stations giving improved central area access or stations related to major destinations. Stations of these types will require demand forecasting techniques that are specifically designed to focus on their key characteristics and are considered beyond the scope of this chapter.

8.2   BR's demand forecasting approaches

Before developing demand forecasting techniques that are specifically concerned with new local services, it is useful to review the development of BR's existing demand forecasting procedures (see also Chapter 3). This can be seen as originating with the Model for Optimising the Network of Inter City Activities (MONICA) which was developed by Tyler and Hassard (1973). This was a direct demand model of London based InterCity flows. However, in application it was found that the model failed to accurately predict the effects of changes in service over time.

As a result, emphasis was placed on the development of specific time-series derived elasticity models (for example, Jones and Nichols, 1983). BR's current demand forecasting approach, entitled MOIRA, incorporates the findings from such studies in order to predict changes in passenger flows as a result of changes to the timetable expressed as a level of service quality index (Whitehead,

1981). However, such an incremental approach can not be applied where existing rail flows are low or zero. This is unlikely to be the case for InterCity services with a coarse zoning system, but is likely to be the case for local services with a fine zoning system. Even if zones are defined so that some relevant rail trips are made in each zone and elasticities are applied to study changes in service, it is likely that changes (for example, in access time) will be so great that the use of constant point elasticities (which only apply to marginal changes) is inappropriate. Hence, the mainstream modelling approach adopted by BR is not really suitable to studying the new services and stations that this chapter is interested in. Trip rate modelling approaches have been developed that might overcome some of these problems (see Chapter 9) but a further problem is that existing approaches have concentrated on Inter City services. There have been few models of local rail demand and those that have been developed tend to concentrate on commuting (Stark, 1981, Glaister, 1983, and see also Chapter 7).

The problems are magnified by the fact that demand forecasting for new rail stations and services is affected by a number of particular difficulties. Investments (particularly in new stations) are relatively small, so cheap forecasting methods are required. Where rail does exist it is often the minority mode so that large (and hence costly) samples are required if Revealed Preference (RP) mode choice models are to be developed (i.e. models based on actual choices). Moreover, locally calibrated RP models cannot be developed for a mode that does not already exist. In addition, it might be expected that new rail stations and services will lead to some generation of demand. Evidence from West Yorkshire and elsewhere confirms this. Hence, the use of mode choice models on their own (i.e. without consideration of trip generation and distribution) is inappropriate, except possibly for studies of the journey to work.

In Section 8.3 a number of possible approaches are investigated that are based on RP data. These include a simple trip rate model, an aggregate direct demand model (which has a precedent in the work of White and Williams (1976)) and a disaggregate mode choice model (which has a precedent in the work of West Midlands County Council (1984)). Disaggregate modelling techniques have also been used to assess rail investment in the U.S. (McFadden et al., 1979) and the Netherlands (Ruhl et al., 1979).

An alternative approach to forecasting the demand at a new station is simply to use market research to ask the question "if a new station was opened at i, with level of service Q, how often, and for what journeys, would you use it?". This approach, which we have termed the Stated Intentions approach, was, in essence, used in other studies to forecast usage at new stations in Scotland and in Somerset. However, such an approach is likely to lead to an overestimate of demand, unless adjusted, as it is prone to a number of biases:

(i)   Self selectivity bias. In a self completion survey, rail users are more likely to return the survey form than non users. To adjust for this bias Heggie and Papoulias (1976) propose that non-respondents should be assumed to be non-users of the new facility.

(ii)   Non commitment bias. Respondents are not committed to behave in the way they have responded. This may be exacerbated by misperceptions. When respondents come to actually use the service they may find the timings inconvenient, the trains overcrowded or unreliable.

(iii) Policy response bias. Respondents may answer strategically in order to achieve the desired policy response (e.g. get the new station opened).

Thus work by Couture and Dooley (1981) showed that in the case of a new transit system in Danville, Illinois such a simplistic approach resulted in a ratio of intended to actual users of three to one. A study of South Wigston station (Leicestershire) indicated that assuming non respondents are non users reduces the bias but predicted usage was still between 38% and 73% higher than actual usage (Hockenhull, 1984). Stated intentions surveys carried out by Network SouthEast have apparently led to similar results.

A more sophisticated approach is based on the Stated Preference (SP) approaches, which in transport applications in Britain were pioneered by BR (Sheldon and Steer, 1982, and see also chapter 4). In fact, SP is a generic term which has been applied to a number of methods of analysing hypothetical choices (see Benjamin and Sen (1982) for a comparison of four techniques). A number of studies have shown that, in providing relative valuations of attributes, SP models perform no worse than RP models and most often perform considerably better (see, for example, Louviere et al., 1981). Their main advantage, as far as this study is concerned, is their ability to assess new facilities. Their main disadvantage is that their use in forecasting is still in its infancy. An SP approach will be developed in Section 8.4.

8.3   Revealed Preference (RP) models

In this section three model types will be developed. They are (in order of increasing complexity): a Trip Rate Model, an Aggregate Simultaneous Model and a disaggregate Mode Choice Model.

Trip Rate Model (TRM)

Surveys of six new stations in West Yorkshire identified two main catchment areas: the 0-800m zone, accounting for 62% of users and with the vast majority walking to the station; and the 800m-2km zone, accounting for 25% of users with the majority still walking.   It is only from beyond 2km that the majority use mechanised access modes (see Table 8.2). It should be noted that the determination of station catchment areas is, in itself, worthy of specialist study (see, for example, Black and Black, 1982). It is a weakness of aggregate procedures that catchment areas have to be pre-defined before we can progress any further.

Table 8.2
Origin access distance by access mode (%)

	% of users	------------------of which------------------				
		Walk	Bus	Car driver	Car pass.	Other
0-800m	62	97	0	1	3	0
801m-2km	25	74	8	8	10	0
Over 2km	13	33	19	17	27	4

Source: Preston, 1987.

The TRM simply expresses station usage as a function of the population within 0-800m and 800m-2km catchment ones, factored up to take into account usage from beyond 2km. Three examples are given in Table 8.3 which indicates that the TRM lacks spatial transferability. This is because it fails to take into account factors such as the socio-economic characteristics of the catchment area population, the attractiveness of destinations, the level of rail service and competition from other modes.

Table 8.3
Trip rate models

	Trips per thousand population		% of users for beyond 2km
	0-800m	800m-2km	
West Yorkshire (1)	126	26	13
South Wigston (2)	181	13	21
Langley Mill (3)	60	17	43

Sources: (1) Preston, 1987
       (2) Mason and Preston, 1987
       (3) Peakall, 1987

Aggregate Simultaneous Model (ASM)

These additional factors were taken into account through the development of a direct demand model which was termed the ASM. This model was calibrated with data on 99 flows estimated from the 1981/2 Passenger Train Surveys for 39 small town, suburban and rural stations in West Yorkshire. Two preferred model forms were developed: a log linear and a semi-log model. These are represented by models 1 and 2 respectively in Table 8.4. The formulations were partly chosen because they reduced problems of multicollinearity and heteroscedasticity. The models only have a moderate goodness of fit, almost half the variation is unexplained. In particular, the ASM underpredicted flows from long established commuter stations. In part, this may be because these commuter stations draw users from beyond 2 kilometres or have, over time, attracted people who, all other things being equal, have a greater than average preference for rail travel. If six outliers of this type were excluded the R^2 of equation 1 increased to 0.66.

Aside from some particular specification and measurement problems, the ASM is affected by problems common to cross sectional models. In particular, it lacks a dynamic structure (which is important when patronage growth over time is considered) and is afflicted by simultaneity problems. The model was also shown to lack temporal transferability. Models 1 and 2 were re-calibrated with 1984 data (based on self completion questionnaires) and, out of 14 parameter values, 5 were shown to have significantly changed their value, at the 5% significance level. Despite these problems, the ASM has been applied to around 80 sites in 12 different counties. It has become evident that its spatial transferability is limited and that it is relatively insensitive to service level changes. These issues will be further examined in Section 6.

Table 8.4
Regression models of rail demand

(t-statistics in brackets)

Dependent variable: LFLOW

Models:	1		2		3	
Intercept	5.496	(3.025)	-1.468	(-0.790)	-3.580	(-2.231)
LOPOP	0.380	(2.617)	0.423	(2.868)	0.562	(3.230)
LOPOP2	0.164	(1.733)	0.147	(1.542)		
LRSOC	0.246	(2.034)	0.248	(2.047)		
LDRX	0.269	(6.678)	0.291	(6.507)		
LREMP					0.252	(4.051)
LGCRA	-1.239	(-4.307)				
GCRA	-0.007	(-3.971)				
LRS			0.574	(3.315)		
LGCOTH	-1.341	(-2.269)	0.507	(1.721)		
LBS			-0.250	(-2.408)		
IC			0.966	(4.634)		
INTOPP					1.247	(-8.077)
R^2	0.539		0.532		0.709	
$\bar{R}^2$	0.509		0.502		0.678	

The variables used in these models are defined in Appendix 8.1.

A possible improvement might be to develop separate models for work and non work journeys (or, alternatively, peak and off peak trips). It was necessary to develop a non work trip model for West Yorkshire, to be used in conjunction with the disaggregate models of work trips described in the next section. This model was calibrated for 64 flows based on 1984 data and is given as model 3 in Table 8.4.

Disaggregate Mode Choice Models (MCM)

As far as this chapter is concerned, an aggregate approach has a number of weaknesses. It fails to establish the importance of factors that exhibit greater intra-zonal variation than inter-zonal variation and this is particularly true of walk and wait time which may be critical in the choice of public transport mode. It fails to take into account micro-level information on economic activity which will clearly affect travel demand. These shortcomings may be overcome by making use of individual data on the times and costs, of the mode actually used and at least one alternative (or preferably a full choice set of alternatives), in order to calibrate a MCM.

A data set of this type was provided by the 1981 West Yorkshire Corridor Study, which collected suitable information on the journey to work as part of a study into the value of time (MVA, ITS, TSU, 1987). The model form chosen was the hierarchical logit (HL). This form was chosen because it overcomes the Independence of Irrelevant Alternatives property which affects the more widely used multinominal logit model (MNL) and precludes the possibility of differential substitutability and complementarity. It was hypothesised that rail users, all other things being equal, are more likely to be drawn from bus than car. This was confirmed by a generalised likelihood ratio test. HL models were estimated indirectly using the BLOGIT package (Crittle and Johnson, 1980), with the composite cost term (or expected maximum utility (EMU)) being calculated with FORTRAN programs. It is acknowledged that direct estimation (or full information Maximum Likelihood) is preferable to indirect estimation (Daly, 1987) but the requisite software was not available.

At the calibration stage problems were encountered in including socio-economic variables. The preferred model was thus market segmented and consisted of an MNL model for non-car-owning households and an HL model for car-owning households. The structure of this model is given by Table 8.5. A model of this form proved very data intensive and sufficient data only existed to validate the model for five new stations and make predictions for a further three potential sites. A simpler formulation is provided by a single market HL model, as shown by Table 8.6. The spatial transferability of the HL/MNL model was tested by applying the model to a different data set. A likelihood ratio test showed that the model was not transferable but, in part, this was due to problems with the quality of the validation data set. It is not the aim of this paper to comment in detail on the models in Tables 8.5 and 8.6, but it should be noted that some perverse results were achieved (e.g. insignificant parameter values and high adjusted rho-squared measures). Such results may be attributed to the fact that, out of necessity, we were using an RP data set of only limited quality.

Table 8.5
Market segmented HL and MNL models

(A)	Non Car Owners		(B)	Car Owners	
Bus Transport	Train	Car Passenger	Car Driver	Car Passenger	Public → Bus Train

	Value (t-stat)		Value (t-stat)
			(i) Upper Split
ASC-Passenger	-0.844 (-1.305)	ASC-Passenger	-0.339 (-0.596)
ASC-Bus	0.427 (1.004)	ASC-Driver	1.597 (2.789)
Wait time	-0.090 (-2.630)	IVT	-0.064 (-3.178)
Walk time	-0.071 (-2.335)	OVT	-0.059 (-1.481)
IVT	-0.029 (-1.339)	Total Cost	-0.013 (-4.176)
Availability	-3.012 (-4.643)	EMU	0.377 (4.996)
$\bar{\rho}^2$	0.500	$\bar{\rho}^2$	0.803
No. obs.	173	No. obs.	721

Notes
ASC = Alternative Specific
 = Constant
IVT = In Vehicle Time
OVT = Out of Vehicle Time
EMU = Expected Maximum Utility
 = $\ln \Sigma_j \exp (U_j)$
U_j = Utility of mode j

(ii) Lower Split

	Value (t-stat)
IVT-Train	-0.111 (-1.785)
IVT-Bus	-0.118 (-2.605)
Walk time	-0.191 (-3.998)
Wait time	-0.276 (-2.565)
Total Cost	-0.067 (-2.196)
$\bar{\rho}^2$	0.574
No. obs.	97

Table 8.6
Single market HL model

(i) Lower Split		(ii) Upper Split	
	Value (t-stat)		Value (t-stat)
Wait time	-0.132 (-3.025)	ASC-Car Driver	2.742 (5.867)
Walk time	-0.184 (-5.221)	ASC-Car Pass.	0.804 (1.962)
IVT-Bus	-0.092 (-3.024)	EMU	0.205 (2.763)
IVT-Train	-0.080 (-2.295)	OVT	-0.067 (-2.698)
Total Cost	-0.044 (-2.490)	IVT	-0.011 (-0.743)
		Total Cost	-0.014 (-6.252)
$\bar{\rho}^2$	0.466	$\bar{\rho}^2$	0.779
No. obs.	179	No. obs.	907

A problem with disaggregate models in forecasting arises because the individual choice estimates have to be expanded over the population of interest in order to obtain a reliable, unbiased forecast of group behaviour. The problem arises because, for non-linear functions such as the logit model, the function of averages of variables is not the same as the average of functions. Hence, use of aggregate data with a MCM calibrated with disaggregate data will lead to systematic biases (Westin, 1974).

A way of using aggregate data in a manner that reduces this problem is the incremental logit model (Kumar, 1980). This model has been extended so as to incorporate an HL structure and accommodate new modes (Koppelman, 1983, Bates, Ashley and Hyman, 1987) and has been termed the Extended Incremental Logit model (EIL). The main advantage of the EIL is that it reduces the data requirements of the MCM to existing modal shares and the differences between the utilities of new and existing public transport modes.

8.4 Stated Preference models

An alternative way of forecasting demand is through the use of SP techniques. Typically, this involves carrying out an SP experiment to develop models of mode choice and then applying these models to O/D matrices of bus and car trips to determine how many trips will divert to rail. This was essentially the approach used in unpublished studies that forecasted the patronage of new rail services in Edinburgh and Staffordshire. The main problem with this approach is that it can not easily accommodate generated trips whilst it will be affected by the aggregation biases discussed in the previous section.

A similar approach has been developed in the study of a new rail service between Leicester and Burton-on-Trent (Preston and Wardman, 1988) and has been refined in a study of a service between Nottingham and Worksop. The work consists of two stages. In the first stage an SI survey is undertaken which collects information on socio-economic characteristics and existing trip patterns as well as intended rail usage. In the Leicestershire study the SI survey involved distribution of questionnaires to all households within 800m and one in four households within secondary catchment areas (normally 800m to 2km, but this was extended in two cases where it was thought the station could serve communities just beyond the 2km threshold). Altogether, 29,873 questionnaires were distributed, with 4,820 returned, representing a response rate of 16%. Following usual procedure, non-respondents were assumed to be non-users.

In a second stage an SP experiment was undertaken. This survey focused on existing bus and car travellers to central Leicester from the outer Leicester suburbs and the Ashby/Coalville area. Altogether, 1,254 individuals were recontacted, of which 638 (51%) returned questionnaires. Each individual was presented with 16 hypothetical times and costs for train and their existing mode and were asked to indicate which mode they would use. The models were calibrated by Maximum Likelihood, with the BLOGIT package again being used. The resultant models of mode choice are given by Table 8.7. Compared to the RP mode choice models that have been developed in this work, the SP models' parameter values have greater statistical significance (although this is, in part, because there are repeat observations for each individual respondent), socio-economic variables can be explicitly included and, because of the orthogonal design, the problems of collinearity between times and cost which appear to have affected the RP models are avoided.

However, there is a problem with SP models that becomes apparent in the forecasting stage. The models are based on binary logit, the coefficients of which are estimated in units of residual deviation i.e. they are estimated as $\Omega\alpha$ where α is an unscaled parameter, Ω is a scalar calculated as $\pi/(\sigma\sqrt{6})$ and σ is the standard deviation of the error differences between modes. A problem arises where σ is not the same as that which would apply to the actual choices being made. This is likely to be the case for SP experiments where uncertainties/difficulties respondents have with hypothetical choices are likely to be greater than those for actual choices. This in turn will reduce the absolute size of parameter values and hence utilities. For example, in binary choice where rail is the minor mode (i.e. it has lower average utility than the other mode in the choice set) this is likely to lead to overestimates of the probability of choosing rail. This example is likely to be typical of the situation considered in this chapter and is an example of what has been termed the scale factor problem (Bates, 1988 and see Section 4.7). Suggested solutions based on re-scaling with RP data or by pivoting around known elasticities or known parameter values are inappropriate in this instance as RP data cannot exist for a new mode and neither will reliable, local parameter/elasticity estimates.

Table 8.7
SP models of mode choice: Leicester - Burton case study

Parameter	Bus-Train model Value	(t-stat)	Car-Train model Value	(t-stat)
ASC (Train)			-1.907	(8.89)
IVT	-0.086	(10.21)	-0.064	(16.96)
OVT$_t$	-0.067	(9.84)	-0.082	(5.69)
OVT$_c$			-0.040	(1.88)
COST	-0.056	(19.61)	-0.035	(17.35)
FREQ$_t$	+1.327	(15.73)	+1.452	(18.72)
FREQ$_b$	-0.863	(3.34)		
MALE	+0.359	(3.70)		
INCOME > £9,999			-0.151	(2.09)
AGE >39			-0.135	(1.90)
LEISURE	-0.189	(1.88)	+0.592	(7.19)
LEICESTER SUBURBS	-1.022	(7.64)	-0.581	(7.08)
$\overline{\rho}^2$	0.25		0.22	
No. obs.	2549		4314	

Notes: OVT$_t$ denotes Out of Vehicle Time for train
OVT$_c$ denotes Out of Vehicle Time for car
FREQ$_t$ and FREQ$_b$ represent the number of trains and buses per hour.

There are two methods by which forecasts can be derived, and which can inform our final forecast:

(i) The *deterministic* method assigns an individual to the mode with the highest utility, given the estimated weights and the costs and times which would prevail for train and bus/car in the situation to be forecast. Aggregate shares are simply the sum of these individual choices.

(ii) The *probabilistic* method calculates the probability of choosing train for each individual given the estimated utility differences for the situation to be forecast. Aggregate shares are simply the sum of individual probabilities.

The two methods give different results. In binary choice, because of the shape of the logit function, if rail is the minor mode (i.e. a share of less than 0.5, which is the case in most choice situations) the probabilistic forecast will be greater than the deterministic.

Where rail is the major mode, the reverse will be true. The deterministic method has an advantage in that, because the scale factor applies equally to all coefficients and hence does not affect relative utilities, the scale factor problem is avoided. The disadvantage is that the deterministic method, by definition, does not include the stochastic component of random utility (i.e. the error term). Clearly, this problem requires further theoretical and practical investigation. Given that the probabilistic forecasts are thought likely to overstate rail's market share and that the deterministic forecasts are thought likely to understate it, it may be argued that these two forecasts bound the actual value. Therefore, an average of these two forecasts may provide a reasonable approximation of the true value. This point is represented empirically in Table 8.8.

Table 8.8
SP estimates of rail shares for the Leicester to Burton corridor

	Bus users	Car users	All users
Probabilistic forecast	0.142	0.162	0.155
Deterministic forecast	0.119	0.089	0.100
Mean	0.131	0.126	0.128

8.5 Comparison of RP methods - West Yorkshire case study

The accuracy of four different forecasting methods were tested for six new stations in West Yorkshire.

(i)   The West Yorkshire TRM, as given by Table 8.3. This is given by column A.

(ii)   The ASM as given by model 1, Table 8.4. This is given by column B.

(iii)   The HL/MNL model (Table 8.5), aggregated by SE. This method produces forecast for work trips only. Non work trips are estimated by model 3, Table 8.4. This is given by column C.

(iv)   The HL model (Table 8.6), aggregated by EIL. Non work trips are again estimated by model 3, Table 8.4. This is given by column D.

Table 8.9
Forecasted weekday usage at new stations

(Initial Usage Indexed as 1.0)

	2nd year usage	3rd year usage	Aggregate		Disaggregate or hybrid	
			A	B	C	D
			TRM	ASM	MNL/HL with SE	HL with EIL
Fitzwilliam	1.56	1.75	1.39	1.31	-	1.84
Deighton	1.98	1.91	1.76	2.72	1.28	1.98
Crossflatts	1.52	1.63	0.80	2.32	1.48	2.03
Slaithwaite	0.73	1.11	0.67	1.22	1.05	0.92
Bramley	0.89	0.86	1.47	1.35	1.71	1.75
Saltaire	1.25	1.48	0.58	1.49	0.99	1.11
RMSE - initial usage			71.3	108.3	78.6	96.9
- second year usage				73.5	93.9	85.8
- third year usage				64.9	105.8	93.6
AD - initial usage			0.422	0.630	0.343	0.540
- second year usage				0.377	0.371	0.312
- third year usage				0.259	0.370	0.316

For definition of RMSE and AD see Appendix 8.2.

Table 8.9 shows that the TRM produces a forecast that is, on average, within 42% of initial usage, with a RMSE of 71 trips. It is, however, a very simplistic approach and is only presented here as a counterpoint to the more sophisticated approaches that have been developed. Of the three remaining approaches the most accurate, at least initially, is the HL/MNL model, which gives predictions, on average, within around 34% of initial usage. It was estimated that the non-work model contributed 75% of this forecasting error. By contrast, the HL model gives predictions within 54% of initial usage, with a RMSE of around 97 trips. This approach is only slightly more accurate than the ASM which gave predictions some 63% above initial usage, with a RMSE of around 108 trips.

With the exception of the TRM (which was based on first year usage), the models examined in Table 8.9 are forms of equilibrium model. From count data, it is apparent that new station usage has been growing in absolute terms. However, this is against a background of increasing rail usage in West Yorkshire, as between 1982 and 1986 demand at 38 existing local stations increased by 48%. In Table 8.9, second and third year usage figures at six new stations are expressed in relation to the overall increase in demand for rail services as a whole. It can be seen that, with the exception of one station, over the first three years demand has grown at a faster rate than that of the network as a whole. Initially, this trend was extrapolated over five years, with the result that demand in year 5 was estimated to be 75% greater than that in year 1. However, later work suggests that real growth at new stations only occurs in the first three years, with usage in year 3 being 35% higher than that in year 1 (Clarke, 1988). Table 8.9 shows that if these dynamics are taken into account the accuracy of the three equilibrium models is broadly comparable in year 2, but by year 3 the ASM appears to be the most accurate, with the forecast being, on average, within 26% of actual usage. The comparable figures for the MNL/HL and the HL models are 37% and 32% respectively. The ASM's better performance over time is possibly due to its ability to incorporate generated trips, particularly for work journeys.

8.6 Comparison of RP and SP methods - Leicestershire case study

In the study of a new rail service between Leicester and Burton-on-Trent a number of different forecasting approaches were compared, although it is not possible to assess their accuracy because the service has not yet been opened. The approaches compared were:

(i)   The ASM, again based on model 1, Table 8.4, but adjusted in the light of findings at South Wigston where it was found that the ASM underpredicted demand by 58%.
(ii) The TRM for South Wigston, as given by Table 8.3.
(iii) The results of the SI survey, assuming that non-respondents are non-users.
(iv) The results of the SI survey, amended in the light of the SP experiment. This was done by using the SP models in Table 8.7 with reported time and cost data to predict individuals' mode choice. This was then compared with what individuals said they would do in the SI survey.

Table 8.10
Comparison of forecasting methods for a new rail service
between Leicester and Burton on Trent (indexed)

ASM S.Wigston	TRM W.Yorks	SI survey	SI survey adjusted by SP		
			DF	PF	Mean
1.00	1.49	3.07	1.86	2.88	2.38

DF = Deterministic forecast, PF = Probabilistic forecast.

The methods are compared in Table 8.10. It can be seen that the lowest demand forecasts are provided by the ASM. In part, this reflects problems with transferability, particularly with respect to the measure of attractiveness of destinations. It may also reflect the fact that a model calibrated for existing rail services may not be appropriate for a new service. The main problem is that the model was calibrated for stations serving small communities. This is reflected by the fact that catchment areas are specified as being highly localised. In reality, catchment area size will vary from site to site rather than be fixed. The assumption of localised catchment areas is appropriate for new stations on existing services as all medium/large communities can be expected to already have stations. However, new stations on new services may well serve medium/large communities. Experience in validating the ASM in West Yorkshire suggests that the model will underpredict usage from such sites.

Compared to the ASM, the South Wigston TRM predicts usage of the service to be 49% higher. As expected, the SI survey indicated that usage would be high, being almost three times the level predicted by the ASM. However, the SP models did suggest that demand would be lower. Based on the mean of the probabilistic and deterministic forecasts, usage from the SP models being between 61% and 94% of that given by the SI survey. If this pattern is repeated for all 18 intermediate stations on the line rather than just the 6 sites that were included in the SP survey, then usage is estimated as being more than double that forecast by the ASM.

Table 8.11
Comparison of price elasticity and the value of in-vehicle time

	ASM		Single market		SP model		
	Log-linear	Semi-log	HL model (Work trips only)		Bus	Car	Total
Rail Price elasticity	-0.83	-0.65	-0.34	Mean	-2.13	-1.49	-1.75
				DF	-2.50	-1.61	-2.00
				PF	-1.76	-1.36	-1.51
Value of Rail IVT	N/A	N/A	2.4 (Bus users)		1.5	1.8	1.7

* IVT = In Vehicle Time, p/min (mid 1987 values)

A further way that the different forecasting approaches may be compared is through a study of the models' elasticities and values of time. This is done in Table 8.11. Deriving price elasticities from the ASM was relatively straightforward, resulting in an elasticity of -0.83 for the log-linear formulation (model 1, Table 8.4) and -0.65 for the semi-log formulation (model 2, Table 8.4). These are within the range used by BR for their Provincial services. The derivation of elasticities from HL models is more complicated but is still feasible (see, for example, McFadden, 1979, pp 313-316). The single market HL model gives a price elasticity of -0.34. This is for work journeys only and is typical of the price elasticities found for commuter rail services. The derivation of elasticities from an SP model is more problematical, due, in part, to the scale factor problem. Elasticity values were derived by examining the effect of small changes in fare on the deterministic and probabilistic forecasts. It was found that, in this case, the deterministic elasticities had greater absolute values than the probabilistic elasticities. The mean of the two elasticity measures is also presented in Table 8.11. The scale factor problem will mean that, given rail is the minor alternative, absolute point elasticities based on the probabilistic forecasts will tend to be underestimates and those based on deterministic forecasts will tend to be overestimates. The mean value, -1.75, seems unrealistically elastic (and the figure is even more elastic for bus users). In part, this is related to the low values of time (see below) and the fact that all users have an alternative to rail that they are currently making use of. It may also be related to problems inherent in an SP approach. For example, SP approaches may not adequately take into account the effect of habit and inertia. A value of in-vehicle time could not be determined from the ASM, and instead the Department of Transport's standard value at the time of the study (2.0 pence per minute at 1987 prices) was used in the generalised cost formulations. Derivation of value of times from an HL model is problematical. In Table 8.11 the only value presented is that of rail in-vehicle time in the lower split of the model. This is valued at 2.4 pence per minute. The derivation of values of time from the binary logit used for the SP model is straightforward and results in values of 1.5 pence per minute for bus users and 1.8 pence per minute for car users (1987 prices). By contrast, the Department of Transport value has been revised upwards to around 3.2 pence per minute (mid 1987 values). Hence, the SP derived values in Table 8.11 appear to be more in line with the old rather than the current Department of Transport values.

8.7 Conclusion

This chapter has identified and developed a wide range of techniques that can be used to forecast the demand for new rail stations and services. In comparing these techniques, it has not been possible to replicate perfect laboratory conditions in which external effects can be controlled for. The approaches we have compared are based on different model formulations (with differing degrees of specification error), calibrated and validated with different data sets (with differing degrees of measurement error).

The conclusion of this chapter is that forecasting models need to be tailored to the situation they are forecasting. The TRM may be adequate for a 'sketch' planning assessment of a very cheap investment (e.g. a single new station). The ASM appears to be adequate for the assessment of relatively cheap investments (such as a series of new stations), particularly if it can be calibrated locally (and computerised ticketing and geographic information systems should make this increasingly possible). Disaggregate techniques should be used for major investments. RP methods can be used to assess a new rail service serving a particular corridor in an area if data already exists for that area or can be easily collected and rail has a significant share in adjacent corridors with similar socio-economic characteristics. SP methods should be used in areas where there are no existing rail services or where a completely new mode, such as light rapid transit, is being introduced.

Given time and data, there are clearly a number of ways that the forecasting approaches described in this chapter could be improved. We have made a number of suggestions as to how the ASM might be improved. We believe that, given increased data availability as a result of improvements in information technology, most authorities responsible for urban rail networks ought to be developing similar models to aid strategic decision making. The largest scope for improvements is, however, in the development of disaggregate techniques. In particular, we believe that there is considerable scope for combining RP and SP approaches. This would allow the scale factor problem to be explicitly examined, whilst exploiting the advantages of SP in terms of data efficiency and the ability to study new choice contexts. Re-scaled SP models could then be used with existing O/D data. If these SP models also explicitly considered generation then they are likely to provide a potential improvement over the SI/SP approach that we have developed.

It should be emphasised that this study has concentrated on the issue of forecasting the usage of new stations and services. In fact, what is normally required is some form of evaluation and if capital grants are required this evaluation will have to be carried out in great detail (Bates and Lowe, 1989). In terms of a financial evaluation, the ASM can predict revenue and hence is adequate. However, if a social evaluation is to be carried out and user and non user benefits need to be calculated then some form of disaggregate modelling system able to predict mode switching would be more appropriate.

Appendix 8.1
The Aggregate Simultaneous Model (ASM): Definition of Variables

A. *All Purposes Model*

L	=	Denotes a logarithm has been taken
FLOW	=	Number of trips from i to j and j to i per average autumn weekday
OPOP	=	Population usually resident within a straight line distance of 800 metres of the station
OPOP2	=	Population usually resident within a straight line distance of 800 metres and 2 kilometres of the station
RSOC	=	Number of residents within social classes 1 and 2 within 800 metres of the station divided by OPOP
DRX	=	Number of work places within 800 metres of the destination station divided by the economically active population
GCOTH	=	Index of competition, expressed as:

$$GCRA/(GCRA + GCBU + GCCA) \qquad \text{(Model 1)}$$
$$GCBU + GCCA \qquad \text{(Model 2)}$$

where:

GCRA	=	Generalised cost of rail = 2 x (walk + wait time) + in-vehicle time + fare/VOT

where:

Walk	=	Access and egress time
Wait	=	Calculated as a function of headway = 3.0 + 0.185 service interval
Fare	=	Half Standard Return
VOT	=	Department of Transport value of behavioural non-working in-vehicle time
GCBU	=	Generalised cost of bus = 2 x (walk + wait time) + in-vehicle time + fare/VOT

where:

Walk	=	Calculated as rail walk time divided by the number of bus stop pairs on competing bus

		routes within 800 metres of a station
Wait	=	Calculated as a function of headway = 1.46 + 0.26 service interval
GCCA	=	Generalised cost of car = in-vehicle time + operating costs/VOT + parking charge/VOT

where:

Operating costs are taken as fuel costs only, assuming fuel consumption of 44 km per gallon in urban conditions and 62 km per gallon in rural conditions.

In-vehicle time based on link flow speeds of 46 kph in urban conditions and 80 kph in rural conditions.

B.   Non Work Trips Model

FLOW	=	Number of non work trips (excluding education) from i to j and j to i per average weekday
OPOP	=	As above
REMP	=	Retail employment within the central area shopping one
RS	=	Rail service frequency during off peak periods (0930-1500 hours and 1800 hours and beyond)
BS	=	Bus service frequency during off peak periods
IC	=	Dummy variable, = 1 for stations serving medium sized towns, with services timetabled to connect with inter city services. Else = 0
INTOPP	=	Proxy variable to take into account the number of competing or intervening variables.

Appendix 8.2
Definition of Goodness of Fit Measures

RMSE = (Root Mean Square Error) = $\sqrt{\Sigma (F-A)^2/n}$

where:

F = Forecast new station daily usage (ons plus offs)
A = Actual new station daily usage
n = Number of observations

AD = (Absolute Deviation) = $\Sigma |F\text{-}A|/\Sigma A$

9 Socio-economic and demographic factors

JULIE RICKARD AND EILEEN HILL

9.1 Introduction

The techniques discussed in earlier chapters of this book are capable of yielding valuable results on many of the major determinants of rail demand, including fare and service quality variables under the control of railway managers, price and quality of the competition and external economic factors. However, they are not very suitable for investigating the influence of socio-economic and demographic factors. This is because such factors change slowly over time, and are highly correlated with other trend-dominated variables such as income and car ownership.

The current chapter, therefore, discusses the development and use of a third set of techniques - trip rate models - which are used to assess demand on a broader scale, concentrating on overall trip making patterns and trends rather than specific changes. Their basis is in the observation that trip rates vary greatly between different groups in the population. Identification of such groups and knowledge of their magnitude in different areas of the country - and at different points in time - can give the planner an estimate of the size of the overall rail market. Such techniques are becoming of particular relevance as planners face a future which will see substantial changes in the population structure including an ageing of the population and a decrease in the proportion of young, potentially more mobile people.

9.2   Trip rate models

Trip rate models, which are often referred to as trip generation models in urban transportation modelling exercises, have generally been treated as the poor relation of the modelling world. In the 1960's and 1970's the other major stages of urban transportation models - distribution, modal split and assignment models - were developed using an impressive armoury of mathematical techniques. Trip rate (or generation) models on the other hand have received comparatively little attention, even though their importance is widely acknowledged.

The principal technique used in British trip rate models was category analysis. This involves the identification of variables representing the characteristics of an individual which the analyst believes were responsible for different levels of trip making. Each variable, even if originally continuous in nature, was divided into a number of classes. The trip rate of each specific cross-classification was calculated from household surveys. Forecasts were then made for the changes in the classifying variables, and the number of trips in each cell for the forecast year was determined.

The method of choosing the cross-classifying variables was generally extremely crude. Stopher and Meyburg (1975) described it as the outcome of a combination of intuition, judgement and simple data analysis. Consequently it is possible that such models did not use the variables, or categories of variables, that would optimally explain the variation between trip rates in the population. In addition, no form of significance testing was generally applied to the results.

A less common alternative methodology was to use Ordinary Least Squares regression techniques (for example in the work carried out by Downes and Gyenes at the Transport and Road Research Laboratory in 1976). Whilst such techniques represent a move towards providing some degree of statistical sophistication to trip rate models, they are not appropriate for the analysis of less frequent inter-urban rail trip making behaviour which does not follow a Normal distribution.

Rickard (1986 and 1988) observed that, on the contrary, inter-urban trip making behaviour can more reliably be described by the Negative Binomial and Poisson distributions. She found that, in aggregate, trip making behaviour in both the business and non-business markets follows a Negative Binomial distribution.

Statistical theory shows that such distributions can result from populations which comprise sub-populations following separate Poisson distributions (Kendall and Stuart, 1958). Rickard found that this was indeed the case with inter-urban trip making behaviour. Both markets were found to consist of a series of distinct subgroups within the population, the trip making frequency of each being statistically different from the others and following its own Poisson distribution.

This observation led to the development of trip rate models, not with Ordinary Least Squares regression which assumes a Normal distribution of trips, but with Poisson regression techniques which reflect the Poisson distribution of trips.

Poisson regression techniques require a logarithmic transformation of the dependent variable to give the linear equation:

$$\ln\lambda_j = \beta_0 + \ln N_j + \beta_1 x_1 + \beta_2 x_2 + \ldots\ldots + \beta_n x_n$$

where

$\ln$	is natural logarithm
λ_j	is the trip rate of subgroup j and also the parameter of the Poisson distribution
N_j	is the number of individuals in subgroup j
$x_1, x_2, x_3 .. x_n$	are the dummy variables representing characteristics of the respondents
$\beta_1, \beta_2, \beta_3 .. \beta_n$	are the estimated parameters for particular dummy independent variables
β_0	is the 'intercept' (or reference group) term
$j = 1 \ldots m$	m is the total number of combinations - that is, if there are five independent variables each with two levels $m = (2^5) = 32$

This is equivalent to a form of loglinear modelling (McCullagh and Nelder, 1983). The equation is estimated iteratively by Maximum Likelihood techniques. A series of models are estimated, each with one term different from the former. The difference in goodness of fit between the models is calculated, and the significance of the improvement of fit between the successive models analysed using chi-square tables. Finally, model residuals are examined to give an indication of whether an appropriate model form has been found.

Trip rate models should be produced from data collected from household interviews as this minimises any bias against those who do not make long distance trips or those who travel infrequently. The surveys need to be very large as inter-urban rail trip making is a comparatively rare event in the majority of people's lives. In addition, collection of data at the respondents' place of residence allows the models to be used in conjunction with the most comprehensive data source on the population of any area - the census - to produce estimates of trip making in that area.

Table 9.1

Parameter estimates of the business trip model

$$\ln \lambda_j = \beta_0 + \ln N_j + \beta_1 S_2 + \beta_2 S_3 + \beta_3 G_2 + \beta_4 R_2$$

deviance = 18.65   df = 19

Category of respondent		Parameter estimate (β_n)	Standard Error of estimate	Ratio (estimate: S.E.)	Anti-log of estimate
Reference group		-6.995	0.222	-31.509	0.001
S_2	Employers and managers in large establishments, self-employed professionals, intermediate non-manual, armed forces, students	1.774	0.184	9.641	5.894
S_3	Employers and managers in small establishments, professional employees	2.412	0.178	13.551	11.156
G_2	Aged 18-54 years	0.869	0.211	4.118	2.385
R_2	District of origin: Metropolitan city centres, London, non-metropolitan urban areas	0.555	0.145	3.828	1.742

Table 9.2

Parameter estimates of the non-business model

$$\ln \lambda_j = \beta_0 + \ln N_j + \beta_1 S_2 + \beta_2 G_2 + \beta_3 A_2 + \beta_4 T_2 + \beta_5 S_2 G_2$$

deviance = 12.69   df = 10

Category of respondent		Parameter estimate (β_n)	Standard Error of estimate	Ratio (estimate: S.E.)	Anti-log of estimate
Reference group		-4.525	0.091	-49.725	0.011
S_2	Professional employees, armed forces, students	0.659	0.148	4.453	1.922
G_2	Aged 18-24 or over 65	0.200	0.087	2.999	1.221
A_2	Resident in district with main line station	0.433	0.088	4.920	1.542
T_2	Household type: 1 adult < 65, 2 adults 65+, >3 adults	0.354	0.079	4.481	1.425
S_2	Membership of groups G_2 S and G	0.767	0.204	3.760	2.153

Rickard estimated the original models on data from the Long Distance Travel Survey (LDTS) for 1978/79. Whilst this data is now clearly dated, it is useful to look at the results because discontinuation of the LDTS has meant that such comprehensive data are not available for more recent years. The data set included approximately 40,000 completed interviews collected from throughout Great Britain.

The final form of the rail business and non-business models is shown in Tables 9.1 and 9.2. Exploratory analysis of the data showed that a division of the non-business market between trips to visit friends and relatives and other leisure trips was not worthwhile, as their composition is very similar.

The parameter estimates in Tables 9.1 and 9.2 can be used to calculate an estimate of the long distance (i.e. over 50 miles) rail trip rate of groups of individuals with each combination of characteristics. The characteristics of the survey respondents are represented as dummy variables in each model. Level 1 of each variable consists of individuals falling into categories of that variable associated with low rail usage. Level 2 (and level 3 where appropriate) represents individuals with high levels of rail usage. The anti-logarithm of the reference group parameter represents the trip rate of individuals categorised as level 1 (i.e. in low rail usage group) for each variable selected. The remaining parameters allow the trip rates of all other groups to be calculated with reference to the reference group.

For example, if an individual is a 30 year old self-employed professional living in the centre of Liverpool, her expected business trip rate can be calculated by adding together the parameter for the reference group and that of S_2, G_2 and R_2 (the high rail usage groups as defined by age socio-economic group, age and district of residence) and taking the anti-logarithm of the result. Alternatively the anti-logarithm of each appropriate parameter can be taken and multiplied together to produce the same result.

9.3 Results of the original 1978/79 model

The rail business model

Socio-economic group, age and district of residence were found to be important in determining long distance rail business trip rates. Socio-economic group has the strongest effect. It represents a classification based on the respondent's occupation. As one would expect, the more senior white collar occupations (employers, managers, professionals and intermediate non-manual workers) have significantly higher trip rates than the remainder of the population. Students and members of the armed forces also fall into this higher usage group as they make above average numbers of trips which they define as 'in course of work' even though they do not fall into the stereotype of the briefcase-carrying business travellers. Two occupational categories - employer/managers in establishments employing less than 25 staff and professional employees - have significantly higher trip rates than the remainder of the group and can therefore be seen as the highest usage group in the model (S_3).

The medium usage group (S_2) is fairly diverse in character. Employer/manager group I (those in establishments with 25 or more employees) are in this group because, although they in aggregate have the highest trip rates, most of their business trips are made by car rather than by rail. These groups have particularly high levels of car ownership, higher than those in the highest rail usage group. Intermediate non-manual workers, by contrast, make fewer business trips overall than the professional and managerial groups but make a relatively high proportion of these (33 per cent) by rail. The comparatively high trip rates of students and members of the armed forces may be partly a function of the availability of railcards, and consequently discounted fares, to these groups.

The age variable is used to divide the population into those who are economically active and those that are not. The high usage group consists of those aged between 18 and 55. Those aged between 16 and 18 and between 55 and 65 do not have sufficiently high business trip rates to warrant inclusion in the high usage group.

The 'type of origin' variable classifies trip rates into two groups by the respondent's district of residence. Those living in the centres of the Metropolitan areas (that is Liverpool, Manchester, Sheffield, Newcastle, Birmingham, Leeds, Glasgow and London) or in other non-metropolitan towns (free standing towns such as Derby, Nottingham, Norwich and Cardiff) form the high usage group. The remainder form the low usage group. A variable representing access to, and quality of, rail service was entered into early attempts to estimate the model but was dropped as it did not represent as much of the variation in the trip rates as the 'type of origin' variable. It is likely, however, that the 'type of origin variable' represents these concepts in addition to characteristics related to type of urban area.

Table 9.3 shows the trip rates that result from the model. Clearly there is much variation. They lie in a range of 0.001 trip per two weeks (or one trip every 38 years!!) to 0.042 (approximately 1 trip a year). Each group contains a variety of individual trip rates (recall from above that each group's trip rates follow a Poisson distribution). The majority of people in each group will make no trips within any particular two week period.

The fifth column of Table 9.3(b) shows each group's average long distance car trip rate for business trips. Note that with only one exception the car trip rates are higher than the corresponding rail trip rates. Employer/managers in small establishments and professional employees aged 18-54 have by far the highest rail trip rates. There is clear evidence, however, that those residing in urban areas have a stronger tendency to use rail, at the expense of car, than those located elsewhere.

Similarly, in the medium rail usage group as defined by SEG (employers/managers of large establishments, self-employed professionals, students and members of the armed forces) there is a clear tendency for those individuals who live in an urban area to substitute rail for car. Indeed, it is for this group that the rail share of the market is highest.

Examination of column 6 of Table 9.3 shows that there is a positive relationship between car trip rate (and to a lesser extent rail trip rate) and the proportion of households in the group that have a car. Furthermore, in the majority of groups those households with a car have higher business trip rates by both modes than those without. It would appear likely, therefore, that car ownership represents an additional, unused, variable such as status in the company. This was not included in the original variable selection as no information of this type was collected in the LDTS.

The rail non-business model

Socio-economic group was also found to be the most important variable determining non-business trip rates. The high usage group consists of professional employees, members of the armed forces and students. The latter two groups can be expected to have relatively high trip rates because they are entitled to buy railcards, thereby having access to discounted fares, frequently spend large parts of the year separated from families and friends and have relatively low levels of car ownership. Professional employees, on the other hand, are members of this group because they generally have above average incomes but have lower car-ownership rates than employer' managers or self-employed professionals. This may be because many do not have the company cars that may be available to these other groups. Consequently, a high proportion of their trips are carried out by rail.

Age of the respondents is also a significant, though secondary, determinant of non-business trip rates. Those aged between 18 and 24 or over 65 years form the higher usage group. Once again, this may be partly the result of the selective availability of railcards for students and senior citizens. The Young Persons railcard was introduced at a later date and can be seen as reinforcing this division. Again, these groups are more likely than others to travel independently so rail travel is comparatively economical for them.

The type of household of which the respondent is part is also important. The high usage group consists of households comprising one adult under 65 years, households of two adults over 65 years and households with more than three adults. Whilst at first sight this appears to be a fairly diverse group, examination of the exploratory analysis shows that indeed this is the most appropriate grouping.

Those aged under 65 and living alone are, by definition, separated by distance, frequently long distance, from friends and relatives and, at the time of the survey, solitary travel made rail travel a more economical option than car travel.

The presence of two-pensioner households in the upper group again appears to be a function of railcard availability. Households comprising one adult aged over 65 are not in this group, however. They have a low average trip rate. It is possible that many of this group are older-than-average pensioners, many of whom have outlived their partners. Advanced age may be an impediment to rail travel for this group.

In the original model, Rickard identified a fourth determining characteristic - the level of accessibility of the individual's district of residence to the rail network. The sample was divided into a high usage group - those who live in a district with a station on a main line service and a low usage group consisting of those who live in districts with a rail feeder service or no service at all.

Table 9.4 shows the trip rates for each of the subgroups identified. Once again, there is much variation with trip rates ranging from an average of 0.010 trip per individual per two week (or one trip every 3.7 years) to 0.126 trips per two weeks (or 1.638 trips per year). Once again the reader is reminded that each of these figures represents an average of a Poisson distribution in which most individuals make no trips in a two week period and others make multiple trips.

The structure of the non-business model is a little more complicated than the business model. It contains a term representing interaction between the socio-economic group and age variables. This means that if an individual is a member of the high rail usage groups as defined by both socio-economic group and age, he or she will have particularly high trip rates. Car ownership was not identified as a significant variable.

Table 9.3a
Subgroups selected by the rail business model

Socio-economic group of respondent	Age of respondent	Type of origin of respondent
B_1	Junior non-manual, not economically active (except students)	Under 18yrs Over 55yrs	Outer metropolitan areas, rural areas
B_2	Junior non-manual, manual, not economically active (except students)	Under 18yrs Over 55yrs	Conurbation central cities, London, other urban areas
B_3	Junior non-manual, not economically active (except students)	18-54yrs	Conurbation central cities, London, other urban areas
B_4	Junior non-manual, manual, not economically active (except students)	18-54yrs	Outer metropolitan areas, rural areas
B_5	Employer/manager group I, self-employed professionals, intermediate non-manual workers, students	Under 18yrs Over 55yrs	Outer metropolitan areas, rural areas
B_6	Employer/manager group I, self-employed professionals, intermediate non-manual workers, students	Under 18yrs Over 55yrs	Conurbation central cities, London, other urban areas
B_7	Employer/manager group I, self-employed professionals, intermediate non-manual workers, students	18-54yrs	Conurbation central cities, London, other urban areas
B_8	Employer/manager group I, self-employed professionals, intermediate non-manual workers, students	18-54yrs	Outer metropolitan areas, rural areas
B_9	Employer/manager II, professional employees	Under 18yrs Over 55yrs	Outer metropolitan areas, rural areas
B_{10}	Employer/manager II, professional employees	Under 18yrs Over 55yrs	Conurbation central cities, London, other urban areas
B_{11}	Employer/manager II, professional employees	18-54yrs	Conurbation central cities, London, other urban areas
B_{12}	Employer/manager II, professional	18-54yrs	Outer metropolitan areas, rural areas

Table 9.3b

Business trip rates associated with groups selected
in the rail business model (S/G/R)

Group Nº	Nº of LDTS respondents in the group	Rail trip rate observed on the LDTS*	Rail trip rate expected from the model*	Nº of rail trips observed on the LDTS	Nº of rail trips expected from the model	Car trip rate observed on the LDTS*	Households with a car (%)	Car trip rates Households without a car	Car trip rates Households with a car	Rail trip rates Households without a car	Rail trip rates Households with a car
B1	6656	0.001	0.001	3	6.1	0.003	51.1	0.001	0.005	0.000	0.001
B2	4251	0.001	0.002	5	6.5	0.003	43.7	0.002	0.005	0.000	0.002
B3	5960	0.005	0.004	28	22.6	0.010	66.1	0.007	0.012	0.005	0.005
B4	10279	0.002	0.002	22	21.8	0.014	73.8	0.002	0.018	0.001	0.002
B5	685	0.005	0.005	4	3.2	0.019	86.1	0.000	0.022	0.000	0.007
B6	403	0.009	0.009	4	3.8	0.005	74.9	0.000	0.007	0.000	0.013
B7	1328	0.020	0.022	26	29.9	0.025	79.2	0.007	0.030	0.028	0.017
B8	1907	0.015	0.013	28	24.6	0.031	98.5	0.009	0.034	0.014	0.015
B9	316	0.020	0.010	7	3.2	0.057	89.2	0.029	0.060	0.000	0.025
B10	192	0.021	0.018	4	3.4	0.042	75.0	0.000	0.056	0.000	0.028
B11	764	0.042	0.042	32	32.5	0.098	83.5	0.016	0.114	0.024	0.045
B12	1349	0.021	0.024	29	32.9	0.108	93.4	0.112	0.108	0.022	0.021
Entire sample	34090	0.006	0.006	192	190.5	0.017	66.0	0.004	0.024	0.003	0.007

Table 9.4a
Subgroups selected by the rail non-business model

Socio-economic group of respondent	Age of respondent	Household type of respondent	Access to rail network/quality of rail service of respondent's home district
NB1 Employer/manager, self-employed professional, intermediate and junior non-manual, manual, not economically active (except students)	Under 18 or 25-64	2 adults or families	Rail feeder or no station
NB2 Employer/manager, self-employed professional, intermediate and junior non-manual, manual, not economically active (except students)	18-24 or over 65	1 adult 65+, 2 adults below retirement age or families	Rail feeder or no station
NB3 Employer/manager, self-employed professional, intermediate and junior non-manual, manual, not economically active (except students)	Under 18 or 25-64	1 adult 65+, 2 adults	Main line station
NB4 Employer/manager, self-employed professional, intermediate and junior non-manual, manual, not economically active (except students)	Under 18 or 25-64	1 adult under 65, large adult households	Rail feeder or no station
NB5 Employer/manager, self-employed professional, intermediate and junior non-manual, manual, not economically active (except students)	Under 18 or 25-64	1 adult under 65, large adult households	Main line station
NB6 Employer/manager, self-employed professional, intermediate and junior non-manual, manual, not economically active (except students)	Under 18 or 25-64	2 adults below retirement age or families	Main line station
NB7 Employer/manager, self-employed professional, intermediate and junior non-manual, manual, not economically active (except students)	18-24 or over 65	1 adult aged 18-24, 2 adults 65+, large adult household	Main line station
NB8 Employer/manager, self-employed professional, intermediate and junior non-manual, manual, not economically active (except students)	18-24 or over 65	1 adult aged 18-24, 2 adults 65+, large adult households	Rail feeder or no station

Socio-economic group of respondent	Age of respondent	Household type of respondent	Access to rail network/ quality of rail service of respondent's home district
NB9 Professional employees, members of the armed forces, students	Under 18, 25-64	2 adults or families	Rail feeder or no station
NB10 Professional employees, members of the armed forces, students	Under 18, 25-64	2 adults or families	Main line station
NB11 Professional employees, members of the armed forces, students	18-24, over 65	1 adult 65+, 2 adults below retire- ment age or families	Rail feeder or no station
NB12 Professional employees, members of the armed forces, students	18-24, over 65	1 adult 65+, 2 adults below retire- ment age or families	Main line station
NB13 Professional employees, members of the armed forces, students	Under 18, 25-64	1 adult, large adult households	Rail feeder or no station
NB14 Professional employees, members of the armed forces, students	Under 18, 25-64	1 adult, large adult households	Main line station
NB15 Professional employees, members of the armed forces, students	18-24, over 65	1 adult aged 18-24, 2 adults 65+, large adult households	Rail feeder or no station
NB16 Professional employees, members of the armed forces, students	18-24, over 65	1 adult aged 18-24, 2 adults 65+, large adult households	Main line station

Table 9.4b
Non-business trip rates associated with groups selected in the rail business model (SG/A/T)

Group Nº	Nº of LDTS respondents in the group	Rail trip rate observed on the LDTS	Rail trip rate expected from the model	Nº of rail trips observed on the LDTS	Nº of rail trips expected from the model	Car trip rate observed on the LDTS	Households with a car (%)	Car trip rates — Households without a car	Car trip rates — Households with a car	Rail trip rates — Households without a car	Rail trip rates — Households with a car
NB1	4856	0.010	0.011	50	52.6	0.087	70.9	0.023	0.092	0.015	0.008
NB2	1176	0.014	0.013	16	15.6	0.039	35.8	0.019	0.076	0.015	0.012
NB3	2281	0.015	0.020	42	46.6	0.050	36.2	0.019	0.104	0.023	0.011
NB4	2880	0.015	0.015	44	44.5	0.077	68.6	0.017	0.104	0.023	0.012
NB5	5887	0.024	0.024	144	140.2	0.079	69.4	0.023	0.103	0.036	0.019
NB6	9025	0.017	0.017	150	150.8	0.093	73.4	0.030	0.116	0.031	0.011
NB7	3995	0.028	0.029	110	116.1	0.057	57.3	0.015	0.088	0.035	0.022
NB8	1897	0.024	0.020	46	37.8	0.055	56.3	0.017	0.084	0.018	0.029
NB9	197	0.020	0.021	4	4.2	0.168	88.8	0.000	0.189	0.000	0.023
NB10	509	0.047	0.032	24	16.4	0.147	88.8	0.140	0.148	0.105	0.040
NB11	38	0.026	0.055	1	2.1	0.184	73.7	0.100	0.214	0.000	0.036
NB12	93	0.097	0.085	9	7.9	0.086	79.6	0.053	0.095	0.158	0.081
NB13	210	0.010	0.030	2	6.3	0.043	83.8	0.000	0.051	0.000	0.011
NB14	547	0.040	0.046	22	25.2	0.135	86.7	0.027	0.152	0.055	0.038
NB15	103	0.055	0.079	6	8.1	0.165	87.4	0.000	0.189	0.000	0.067
NB16	396	0.126	0.121	50	47.9	0.109	79.0	0.036	0.128	0.157	0.118
Entire sample	34090	0.021	0.021	720	722.2	0.062	66.0	0.017	0.086	0.028	0.017

The highest rail trip rates are recorded by students, professional employees and members of the armed forces aged between 18 and 54 and either living alone or living in households with more than three (possibly economically independent) adults. This group appear to be particularly sensitive to accessibility to the rail network. If they live in a district with a main line rail service they make more trips by rail than by car. If they live in a district with an inferior service the opposite applies. Once again, there is a positive relationship between the proportion of the group that live in households with a car and the group's car trip rate. However, there is also a relationship with their rail trip rates. Groups with below-average rail trip rates have a broad range of levels of car ownership. This includes those low car-owning households that have low trip rates by both modes and those high car owning groups that have high trip rates by car. As with business trips, households with access to a car generally have higher car trip rates than those without. Conversely, the majority of them have lower rail trip rates than households without cars. Six groups do have higher rail trip rates among those with cars than those without; but little should be read into this finding, as in each case the number without a car is very small, so there is increased probability that a spuriously high trip rate has been produced by chance.

9.4   Validation of the trip rate models

Before any model can be used to produce credible predictions of trip-making behaviour, it should be validated against at least one other data source. The Rickard models have been validated in two separate exercises: against cross-sectional data for five counties of England in 1985 (Rickard, Fowkes and Nash, 1987) and against data from the other Long Distance Travel Surveys carried out in the 1970's and the 1985/86 National Travel Survey (Hill, Rickard, Nash and Fowkes, 1989).

In the first exercise the models were used in conjunction with census data to produce estimates of the levels of long distance trip making in the individual districts of Greater Manchester, West Yorkshire, Surrey, Hertfordshire and Lincolnshire. This was a straightforward exercise: the appropriate trip rates from Tables 9.3 and 9.4 were multiplied by the number of individuals known to be in each group in the appropriate district, as given by the 1981 census. The trips produced for each subgroup were then summed to give the number of trips expected in a district.

These figures were subsequently tested against observed trip rates for the counties. Such data is sparse because, as is explained above, it requires a large (and expensive) sample from a household survey. However, two sources were used: the LDTS itself and British Rail's Area Travel Surveys.

Neither data set gave reason to doubt the predictions of the models. Whilst it is not usually good practice to validate a model on the data source which was used in its development, as this could favour the model being tested and thereby lead to acceptance of a poor model, in this case the problems are minimised by estimating the models on the entire data set and validating them on geographically selected parts of the data. Insufficient sample sizes for the LDTS made validation at the district level impracticable. However, statistical tests show that the models are consistent with the observed trips at County level.

It is interesting to note that there is a large degree of variation between the trip rates of the areas and that this does indeed appear to reflect their socio-economic composition and age structure. The highest predicted business trip rates are in Surrey (6.29 trips per thousand) and Hertfordshire (5.41 trips per thousand) which have relatively high proportions of their population in high trip-making occupations. Manchester, Leeds and Lincoln (which all fall into the 'urbanised' category) all have considerably higher trip rates than the other districts in their respective counties. Similarly, there is a large range in non-business trip rates. In this case, there is less geographical variation in the socio-economic categories used, although there is a slight tendency for the Home Counties to have a higher proportion of high trip making socio-economic groups. It appears that the main differences between districts are accounted for by differences in levels of access to the main line, but that socio-economic group and age do also affect the trip rates of some districts.

The second exercise involved a test of the short term stability of the models. The models were tested against LDTS data for years other than the year on which they were estimated (i.e. 1974/75, 1975/76 and 1976/77). This gives a total sample size in the region of 100,000 people. The trip rates obtained for the same group for different years give an indication of:

1. whether the degree of variation between the different years is sufficiently small to allow the use of 'pooled' estimates for these groups in a subsequent predictive exercise; and

2. whether there is any discernable trend over this relatively short period of time in trip-making by particular groups within the population.

With a couple of exceptions, the trip rates for the different age and SEG categories used in the business model are stable over the four surveys. Furthermore, the differences between the trip rates of the high and low usage groups for each variable were all strongly statistically significant using data pooled for all the years and, in all except two cases, when using data for individual years.

The role of the urbanisation variable, however, was a little surprising. Previous years' data did not show a significant degree of variation between the variables' high and low rail usage groups. However, the differences were significant in the 'pooled' data.

Hill et al.'s conclusions were that the samples from the four LDTS surveys were sufficiently similar, and year on year variations sufficiently small to use the models, with pooled trip rates, to make forecasts. They did, however, adapt the type of area variable to reflect the trip-making behaviour more accurately in the pooled sample.

In contrast to the stability of the business trip rates, a strong between-years variation in the level of trip making for all the non-business subgroups was observed, sufficient to be statistically significant in many cases. The variation is not unexpected, as non-business rail travel is known to be sensitive to fluctuating economic factors, such as rail fare and the state of the economy. It is encouraging, however, that the pattern of trip rates found in each year was similar, with high usage groups making significantly more trips than low usage groups. In fact, significance tests show that the difference between the trip rates for the 'high' and 'low' usage groups for each variable were strongly significant when using both a pooled data set, and in the majority of cases, using each year's data individually.

Hill et al. carried out an additional validation to establish whether trip making behaviour patterns remained stable into the 1980's. They compared special tabulations derived from the Department of Transport's 1985/86 National Travel Survey (NTS) with trip rates derived from the LDTS in the late 1970's. Whilst there are important differences in the way the two surveys were conducted (including the definition of a long distance trip and the period of recall required by the respondent), attempts were made to make the figures comparable, and the conclusion was that the distinction between high-usage and low-usage groups on the variables identified in the Rickard models remains generally valid in the longer term, despite the fact that the level of the non-business travel per head fluctuates considerably.

9.5 The use of the models to forecast future levels of long distance trip-making

Reliable long term forecasts from trip rate models are the product of two elements: reliable trip rate models and reliable forecasts of the individual variables used in the models. Clearly even the most carefully validated model will be of only limited value if it is used with poor population projections. Whilst use of census data means that this is not a problem when using the models to estimate trip rates in areas of unknown market potential at the present time, it can be a greater issue for long term forecasting.

In a recent forecasting exercise, Hill, Rickard, Nash and Fowkes (1989) adapted the original models to make maximum possible utilisation of the demographic data available for forecasting. They concluded that the variables used for analysing long distance rail business travel in the original model could also be used for forecasting, subject to the replacement of the two level location variable by a three level variable related to rail accessibility. In the non-business case, a five variable split was derived. The age variable was refined to give three categories: a high usage group (16-24 and 60-74 years), a medium usage group (25-59 years) and a low usage group (over 74 years). As in the original work, the new high usage group includes those eligible to purchase a railcard to give them access to discounted rail travel, but now excludes those aged 75 and over who were found in the NTS to have a very low trip rate. For rail access, the same three level variable was adopted as for business travel. The two level SEG and household type variables were kept in their original form. Finally, the groups were split between those with, and without, a driving licence. The only exception to this is the group comprising those over 75 which is split by rail access only.

The projections of long distance rail travel were derived from disaggregation of the official forecasts (obtained from the OPCS, the Welsh Office and the Registrar General for Scotland) into the subgroups described above, and application to them of trip rates derived from the 1985/86 National Travel Survey, using relationships found in the earlier LDTS data.

1985 was taken as the base year, and estimates of levels of trip making for 1991, 2001 and 2011 were derived for England and Wales. Figures for Scotland, and therefore Great Britain, are not available for 2011. The projections show the changes in demand which could be expected to arise from changes in the population structure (Table 9.5). The effect of changes in the trip rates of individual subgroups, for whatever reason, have to be superimposed on the changes projected in the tables.

Business travel is projected to continue to increase over the forecasting period, with most growth occurring in the late 1980's. This is principally due to increases in the proportion of the population who fall into the high rail-usage age groups. There is little change in the distribution of the population by SEG or rail access groups.

Non-business travel is expected to fall slightly from its 1985 levels by 1991, remain constant until 2001, and then recover to somewhat above the 1985 level by 2011. These changes are also largely the result of shifts in the age distribution of the population. The shift from high rail usage to medium rail usage groups in the 1990's is reversed after 2001 as a relatively high proportion of the population reach their teens and twenties and the number of young pensioners rises.

If one takes the two markets together, therefore, in this base case the effect of population changes on demand for long distance rail travel can be viewed as largely neutral, with a slight increase predicted by 2011. Business trips could be expected to account for a growing proportion of total trips until the turn of the century, with a slight reduction thereafter.

Table 9.5
Summary results of base projections:
effect of population change on long distance rail travel

	Index of Trips			
England and Wales	1985	1991	2001	2011
Business	100	104	105	106
Non-business	100	98	98	101
Both purposes	100	100	100	102
Percentage of total				
Business	22%	23%	24%	23%
Non-business	78%	77%	76%	77%

Clearly, a high degree of uncertainty must be attached to any long term forecast. Consequently, Hill et al. presented their results in terms of a series of alternative scenarios. The two assumptions which they considered most important to examine were those on SEG and driving licence holding (see Table 9.6). SEG is of central importance as it was identified in the original model as the most important factor in determining both business and non-business trip rates and is clearly subject to change in the light of social and economic changes in society. Licence holding was expected to be subject to major changes over the forecasting period.

Table 9.6
Effect of changing SEG and licence scenarios

Index of Trips

England and Wales	1985	1991	2001	2011
Business travel				
Base scenario	100	104	105	106
Alternative SEG scenario	100	101	102	103
Non-business travel				
Base scenario	100	98	98	101
Alternative SEG scenario	100	98	97	101
Alternative licence scenario	100	95	94	97
Alternative SEG and licence scenario	100	95	93	97
Total travel				
Base scenario	100	100	100	102
Alternative SEG scenario	100	99	99	102
Alternative licence scenario	100	97	96	99
Alternative SEG and licence scenario	100	96	95	98

In brief, the alternative SEG scenario allows for change between each pair of dates (1985-91, 1991-2001 etc.) equivalent to the rate experienced between 1971 and 1981. The numbers of students are assumed to be a fixed proportion of the population aged 16 to 24. The number in the armed forces is assumed to be unchanged throughout. The alternative driving licence scenario assumes further increases in the licence holding of successive cohorts in the population as well as the changes that will occur when existing licence patterns are carried forward into later life.

The principal effect of the alternative SEG scenario is to reduce the projected levels of growth in rail business travel as a proportion of the population shift from the high usage group to the medium usage group. There is very little effect, however, on non-business travel by rail. The overall effect, therefore, is a small fall in the total market in 1991 and 2001.

By contrast, the effect of changing driving licence assumptions on the non-business market is pronounced. There is a greater fall in the market in 1991 and 2001 and the recovery of 2011 is no longer sufficient to regain 1985 levels of patronage.

If the two alternative scenarios are combined, the effect of the SEG changes on business travel, and of the licence holding changes on non-business travel, produce a small drop in projected total travel.

9.6   Discussion of the role of inter-urban rail trip rate models

The principal contribution of the inter-urban trip rate models discussed in this chapter is to draw attention to factors outside the control of the transport operator that determine levels of trip making. Factors such as socio-economic group, age, household structure and geographical location largely determine an individual's need and ability to travel. For example they determine his or her ability to pay, whether a car is available for the journey and the chances that he or she will need to make a business journey. Insights into the role of these factors have an obvious value when one is considering the rail market potential of an areas not currently served by the rail system or in an area which is considered to be underperforming. Rickard, Nash and Fowkes (1987) found that the trip rates in Surrey fall into the latter category; the socio-economic characteristics of the area suggested that it should have higher trip rates than it does, principally as a result of its poor levels of access to the main InterCity rail network.

A second application is to predict the effects of demographic change on future levels of demand. In the application discussed above, Hill, Rickard, Nash and Fowkes (1989) used them to produce forecasts of the levels of inter-urban rail demand until 2011. They have, however, stressed that the models should act merely as a guide to the underlying demographic trends and that other factors, not taken into account in the models, such as fares, level of service, the geographical dispersion of the population, changes in the role of women, the effects of traffic congestion on car use and a possible need to gain the environmental advantages of rail use may have substantial effects on the trends identified.

The results of trip rate models need to be brought together with those of elasticity models to forecast in circumstances in which fares, service levels and competition are also predicted to change.

10 Conclusion

TONY FOWKES

10.1 Overview

In this book we have looked at a variety of means of getting to understand the demand for passenger rail travel. In this chapter we will try to draw some general lessons and give our view as to where attention should be focused in the future. Clearly, there will be continual development in the methods, as well as changes in the relative importance of the underlying parameters to be estimated, and in the contexts for which it is required to understand and forecast rail travel demand. Where possible in this book we have given illustrative examples of parameters estimated for U.K. rail travel demand. These have been far from a complete description of the state of current knowledge since much research is regarded as commercially confidential. We have instead tried to provide a comprehensive exposition to the methods currently in use, although even here commercial confidentiality has impinged and we have omitted mention of some specialist techniques whose usefulness is not yet widely accepted in the U.K. transport planning community.

It is our view that for the art/science of rail travel demand forecasting to develop, and for new methods to gain acceptance by those controlling the all-important investment decisions, there needs to be a considerable degree of openness on the part of those funding research. At least in the initial judgement on new methods this will entail the publishing not just of the methods but the analysis and results too. We hope that the present volume has helped to lift the veil on some of the new methods, and will help to focus attention on what now needs to be done. Before turning to the future, however, let us consider the value of the methods presented earlier.

10.2 A comparison of the value of the various methods of demand analysis

Like all decisions, the choice of a method of demand analysis depends on the associated costs and benefits. On the cost side, some methods (e.g. ticket sales analysis) use data which has already been collected. If this is already resident in the computer to be used for analysis, and has been sufficiently 'cleaned', then the cost can be taken at zero. Other analysis methods will require fresh sampling, the cost of which will rise with the sample size. Despite the usual presence of some fixed cost of sampling, a point will eventually be reached when the extra benefit of increased sample size will be outweighed by the cost. This is because, (a) there will be decreasing returns to extra accuracy, and (b) the extent of the extra sampling accuracy rises only with the square root of the sample size (i.e. an accuracy of $\pm 10\%$ can be improved to $\pm 5\%$ by quadrupling the sample size, generally speaking, in situations where the inaccuracy is solely due to sampling error).

However, not all inaccuracy is usually due to sampling error, so a consideration of methods of demand analysis must also consider the scope for (a) measurement/reporting error (potentially very considerable for Revealed Preference reported values for 'rejected' modes); (b) inherent variability in the quantity being measured (e.g. if demand varies seasonally, increasing the size of a sample taken in November will have relatively little effect in increasing the accuracy of a forecast for February); and (c) biased responses, possibly deliberate (e.g. Stated Intention surveys of the demand for new rail services invariably overstate the actual usage once opened).

In choosing a method of demand analysis we should consider the particular context; how much detail is required; what accuracy is required; what past information is available; and what resources are available? We should not fall into the trap of thinking that a 'desk job' takes no resources while a fresh survey takes massive resources. Desk jobs relying on already collected data may require this data to be provided to the computer to be used for the analysis (which for large data sets may require time from scarce computer systems experts, which may only become available after significant delay) and when the data arrives it may be impossible to satisfactorily 'clean' it. Conversely, it does not take much in the way of resources (for railway employees at least) to count train loadings, obtain recent ticket sales data, or administer simple surveys of passengers.

The approach supported in this book is the one adopted by B.R., namely that research is conducted on the major parameters using the best techniques available in each case, and the evidence then made available to other users. For example, the opportunity afforded by the introduction of High Speed Trains on certain B.R. routes in the 1970's was used in Before and After comparisons in order to estimate, inter alia, the effect of journey time reductions. This was then made available for use in forecasting the effects of journey time changes on other services, in the form of a journey time elasticity. In other situations, much less is assumed transferable over time and from place to place. For example, the forecasting of demand at new or reopened passenger stations generally requires a specific surveying exercise in that locality. However, as we have seen in Chapter 8, a range of alternatives to this are available. If the resources to be devoted to the forecast are very limited then crude trip rate models are available which, given appropriate population data, will permit a rough end ready forecast to be made.

For the larger one-off studies, usually concerning the estimation of one of the major parameters, we have seen that there are two ways to proceed. On the one hand we can study aggregated data, for example of ticket sales at a time when something interesting is happening, or else we can study disaggregate data on particular decisions (either actual or hypothetical). The choice of which method or methods to use is usually indicated by the circumstances, but there is sometimes scope for real choice. It is hoped that this book will have helped the reader to see when each method is indicated, and to gauge the relative merits of each method where there is a real choice.

10.3 What have we learnt about rail demand?

Despite the commercially confidential nature of much of the work in this area, we have been able to present results, mostly arising from work done at the University of Leeds, which throw

174

considerable light on the determinants of the demand for rail travel. Chapter 9 gave evidence on the rail trip rates, for business and leisure, in the U.K. in 1978/79. Considerable detail was presented concerning variations in trip rates with socio-economic factors. The implications of projected demographic changes on rail travel was also analysed.

Chapter 8 looked at how we might forecast usage of new stations and services. A range of methods have been used in a series of case studies in the U.K., usually funded by the local authorities. Again trip rates are investigated, but there is also deeper analysis of whether trips are generated or switched from some other mode of transport. This requires a good understanding of the underlying situation, and much relevant detail is presented in Chapter 8, although we would caution against transferring the results without due care and consideration.

Chapter 7 looked specifically at commuting and in particular at the interaction of the characteristics (e.g. price, speed, service quality) of the transport system with 'land use variables', e.g. the locations of jobs and houses. Special attention is paid to London, which is by far the most important conurbation in the U.K. in terms of rail and commuting. Much detail from surveys and the output from simple models is presented.

Chapter 6 looked at business travel. This is difficult to analyse since the travel decisions are split between the firm, which may have a travel policy of various sorts, and the individual traveller who may have considerable control over his choices without having to meet the financial cost. On the basis of surveys of business travellers and their firms, considerable insight is gained and presented.

Chapter 5 looked at leisure travel, a term encompassing all travel not either commuting to work or travelling in the course of work. Consequently it covers a large variety of reasons for travel. On the basis of surveys of travellers, considerable detail is given of how much they value the main components of rail travel.

10.4 The future

Considerable effort, much of it unpublished, has recently been directed to improving the understanding of the demand for rail travel. This work is continuing. The use of ticket sales data is increasing again now that more reliable data is coming on stream, over a reasonable period, from B.R.'s new APTIS ticket machines. Control flow techniques are being refined, bringing them closer to mainstream econometric methods. Disaggregate modelling techniques are being applied to a wider range of problems. In particular, Stated Preference techniques are being continually developed and used in new ways. Particular attention is being paid now to the forecasting of generated travel, as opposed to travel which is gained to rail from some other mode.

The questions to be asked in the future appear more concerned with expansion and grand schemes. Many stations and services have recently opened, as was discussed in Chapter 8. On the Continent there are many High Speed Lines either under constriction or firmly planned. These involve speeds much greater than current in the U.K. In this context there is therefore much consideration of how such schemes can be justified, in view of the higher energy costs of high speed and the high cost of building the new track alignments usually required. Where Public Enquiries into the scheme are needed, research projects are set up to provide a watertight case as to the justification of the scheme.

The growth of environmental concern is a two-edged sword. As a basic means of moving people, there is no doubt that rail is energy efficient, and so from this point of view should have a rosy future if environmental considerations halt the increase in car usage. However, the case is much less clear cut for High Speed Lines unless considerable traffic is taken from air or car. This is because high speeds are relatively energy inefficient if the alternative is a medium speed train. This highlights the need for better information on cross elasticities between modes for inter-city traffic, and work at the Institute is now concentrating on this issue.

It will be important in the future to understand what potential rail travellers want in terms of price, speed, frequency, reliability and quality of rolling stock. If railways go too 'up market' the mobility of poor non-car-owning households may be impaired. If the railways are dogged by a basic, dirty 'public transport' style image, it will rightly be difficult to tempt motorists from their comfortable cars. If we are to make sensible decisions about the passenger rail services we should have in the future, we need to have a good understanding of what potential passengers want and are prepared to pay for. We hope that this book will both help to spread wider the current state of knowledge, and stimulate further development of the methods of demand analysis.

References

Chapter 2

Evans, A. (1969), 'InterCity Travel and the LM Electrification', Journal of Transport Economics and Policy

Fowkes, A.S., Nash, C.A. and Whiteing, A.E. (1985), 'Understanding Trends in InterCity Rail Traffic in Great Britain', Transportation Planning and Technology

Jones, I. and Nichols, A. (1983), 'Demand for InterCity Rail Travel', Journal of Transport Economics and Policy

OECD (1977), 'The Future of European Passenger Transport', OECD, Paris

Owen, A. and Phillips, G.D. (1987), 'The Characteristics of Railway Passenger Demand', Journal of Transport Economics and Policy

Sheldon, R.J. and Steer, J.K. (1982), 'The Use of Conjoint Analysis in Transport Research', PTRC Summer Annual Meeting

Shilton, D. (1982), 'Modelling the Demand for High Speed Rail

Services', Journal of the Operational Research Society

Tyler, J. and Hassard, R. (1973), 'Gravity/Elasticity Models for the Planning of the Inter Urban Rail Passenger Business', PTRC Summer Annual Meeting

Whitehead, P. (1981), 'Estimating the Effect on Revenue of Rail Service Changes', PTRC Summer Annual Meeting

Wootton, H.J. and Pick, G.W. (1967), 'A Model for Trips Generated by Households', Journal of Transport Economics and Policy, vol. 1, pp. 137-153

Chapter 3

Evans, A. (1969), 'Inter City Travel and the LM Electrification', Journal of Transport Economics and Policy

Fowkes, A.S., Nash, C.A. and Whiteing, A.E. (1985), 'Understanding Trends in Inter-City Rail Traffic in Great Britain', Transportation Planning and Technology, (10), pp. 65-80

Jenkins, G.M., Abbie, E.G., Everest, J.T. and Paulley, N.J. (1981), 'Rail and Air Travel between London and Scotland, Analysis of Competition using Box-Jenkins Methods', TRRL Report LR978, Transport and Road Research Laboratory, Crowthorne

Jones, I.S. and Nichols, A.J. (1983), 'Demand for Inter-City Rail Travel', Journal of Transport Economics and Policy

Leake, G.R. (1971), 'Interurban Mode Choice', University of Leeds

McLeod, G., Everest, J.T. and Paulley, N.J. (1980), 'Analysis of Rail and Air Passenger Flows between London and Glasgow using Box-Jenkins methods', TRRL Report SR524, Transport and Road Research Laboratory, Crowthorne

Owen, A.D. and Phillips, G.D.A. (1987), 'The Characteristics of Railway Passenger Demand', Journal of Transport Economics and Policy

Shilton, D. (1982), 'Modelling the Demand for High Speed Rail Services', Journal of the Operational Research Society

Tyler, J. and Hassard, R. (1971), 'Development of Traffic Generation/Distribution Models in British Rail and their Application to Forward Planning', in PTRC *Models of Traffic Outside Towns*, London

Tyler, J. and Hassard, R. (1973), 'Gravity/Elasticity Models for the Planning of the Inter Urban Rail Passenger Business', PTRC Summer Annual Meeting

Chapter 4

Bates, J. (1988), 'Econometric Issues in Stated Preference Analysis', Journal of Transport Economics and Policy, 22, pp. 59-69

Bates, J.J. and Roberts, M.R. (1983), 'Recent Experience with Models Fitted to Stated Preference Data', proceedings of Seminar M, PTRC Summer Annual Meeting, Brighton

Beggs, S., Cardell, N.S. and Hausman, J. (1981), 'Assessing the Potential Demand for Electric Cars', Journal of Econometrics 16, pp. 1-9

Ben Akiva, M. and Lerman, S. (1985), 'Discrete Choice Analysis: Theory and Applications to Travel Demand', M.I.T. Press, Cambridge, Mass

Benjamin, J. and Sen, L. (1982), 'Comparison of the Predictive Ability of Four Multiattirbute Approaches to Attitudinal Measurement', Transportation Research Record 890, pp. 1-6

Bovy, P.H.L. and Bradley, M.A. (1985), 'Route Choice Analysed with Stated Preference Approaches', Transportation Research Record 1037, pp. 11-20

Bradley, M. (1988), 'Realism and Adaptation in Designing Hypothetical Choice Concepts', *Journal of Transport Economics and Policy*, vol. 22, pp. 121-137

Broom, D., Lowe, S.R., Gunn, H.F. and Jones, P.M. (1983), 'Estimating Values of Time: An Experimental Comparison of Transfer Price Methods with the Revealed Preference Approach', Presented to Seminar N, PTRC Summer Annual Meeting, Brighton (N.B. not in Proceedings)

Chapman, R.G. and Staelin, R. (1982), 'Exploiting Rank Ordered Choice Set Data within the Stochastic Utility Model', Journal of Marketing Research 19, pp. 288-301

Chatterjee, A., Wegmann, F.J. and McAdams, M.A. (1983), 'Non-Commitment Bias in Public Opinion on Transit Usage', Transportation 11, pp. 347-60

Couture, M.R. and Dooley, T. (1981), 'Analysing Traveller Attitudes to Resolve Intended and Actual Use of a New Transit Service', Transportation Research Record 794, pp. 27-33

Fowkes, A.S. (1986), 'The UK Department of Transport Value of Time Project: Results for North Kent Commuters using Revealed Preference Methods', International Journal of Transport Economics 13, pp. 197-207

Fowkes, A.S. (1991), 'Recent Developments in Stated Preference Techniques in Transport Research', PTRC Summer Annual Meeting, University of Sussex

Fowkes, A.S. and Tweddle, G. (1988), 'A Computer Guided Stated Preference Experiment for Freight Mode Choice', Transportation Planning Methods, Code P306, proceedings of PTRC-SAM, Planning and Transportation Research and Computing, London, pp. 295-305

Fowkes, A.S. and Wardman, M.R. (1988), 'Design of SP Travel Choice Experiments, with special reference to Taste Variations', Journal of Transport Economics and Policy, 22, pp. 27-44

Green, P.E. and Srinivasen, V. (1978), 'Conjoint Analysis in Consumer Research: Issues and Outlook', Journal of Consumer Research 5, pp. 103-123

Gunn, H.F. (1984), 'An Analysis of Transfer Price Data', Proceedings of Seminar H, PTRC Summer Annual Meeting, Brighton

Hensher, D.A. (1976), 'The Value of Commuter Travel Time Savings: Empirical Estimation using an Alternative Valuation Model', Journal of Transport Economics and Policy 10, pp. 167-176

Hensher, D.A. and Truong, T.P. (1983), 'Values of Travel Time

Savings from a Revealed Preference Approach and a Direct Experimental Approach', Research Paper 269, School of Economic and Financial Studies, Macquarie University, Australia

Kocur, G., Hyman, W. and Aunet, B. (1982a), 'Wisconsin Work Mode-Choice Models Based on Functional Measurement and Disaggregate Behavioural Data', Transportation Research Record 895, pp. 25-31

Kocur, G., Adler, T., Hyman, W. and Aunet, B. (1982b), 'Guide to Forecasting Travel Demand with Direct Utility Assessment', United States Department of Transportation, Urban Mass Transportation Administration, Report no. UMTA-NH-11-0001-82-1, Washington D.C.

Lee, N. and Dalvi, M.Q. (1969), 'Variations in the Value of Travel Time', Journal of the Manchester School of Economics and Social Studies 37, pp. 213-36

Lee, N. and Dalvi, M.Q. (1971), 'Variations in the Value of Travel Time: Further Analysis', Journal of the Manchester School of Economics and Social Studies 39, pp. 187-204

Leigh, T.W., McKay, D.B. and Summers, J.O. (1984), 'Reliability and Validity of Conjoint Analysis and Self Explicated Weights: A Comparison', Journal of Marketing Research 21, pp. 456-62

Levin, P., Louviere, J.J., Schepanski, A.A. and Norman, K.L. (1983), 'External Validity Tests of Laboratory Studies of Information Integration, Organisational Behavioural and Human Performance', vol. 31

Louviere, J.J. (1988), 'Conjoint Analysis Modelling of Stated Preferences', Journal of Transport Economics and Policy, 22, pp. 93-119

Louviere, J.J. and Kocur, G. (1983), 'The Magnitude of Individual Level Variations in Demand Coefficients: A Xenia, Ohio Case Example', Transportation Research 17A, pp. 363-373

McFadden, D. (1974), 'Conditional Logit Analysis of Qualitative Choice Behaviour", in Zarembka, P. (ed) "Frontiers in Econometrics", Academic Press, New York

McFadden, D. (1981), 'Econometric Models of Probabilistic Choice', in Structural Analysis of Discrete Data with Econometric Application, Manski, C.F. and McFadden, D. (eds.), MIT Press, Cambridge, Mass, pp. 198-272

McFadden, D, and Reid, F. (1974), 'Aggregate Travel Demand Forecasting from Disaggregate Behavioural Models', Transportation Research Record 534, pp. 24-37

Moore, W.L. (1980), 'Level of Aggregation in Conjoint Analysis: An Empirical Comparison', Journal of Marketing Research 17, pp. 516-23

MVA Consultancy, Institute for Transport Studies, University of Leeds and Transport Studies Unit, Oxford University (1983), 'Progress Report for Meeting on 22 November 1983', Value of Time Study Report, Prepared for APM Division, Department of Transport, Unpublished

MVA Consultancy, Institute for Transport Studies, University of Leeds and Transport Studies Unit, Oxford University (1987), 'The Value of Travel Time Savings', Policy Journals, Newbury, Berkshire

Ortuzar, J. de D. and Ivelic, A.M. (1987), 'Effects of Using More Accurately Measured Level of Service Variables on the Specification and Stability of Modal Choice Models', Proceedings of Seminar C, PTRC-SAM, London

Preston, J. (1987), 'The Evaluation of New Local Rail Stations in West Yorkshire', PhD Thesis, Institute for Transport Studies, University of Leeds, unpublished

Richards, M.G. (1980), 'Can Disaggregate Models Improve our Forecasting Approach', in International Conference on Research and Applications of Disaggregate Travel Demand Models, University of Leeds

Timmermans, H. (1984), 'Decompositional Multiattribute Preference Models in Spatial Choice Analysis: A Review of Some Recent Developments', Progress in Human Geography 8, pp. 189-221

Wardman, M.R. (1988), 'A Comparison of Revealed Preference and Stated Preference Models of Travel Behaviour', Journal of

Transport Economics and Policy, 22, pp. 71-91

Wardman, M.R. (1991), 'Stated Preference Methods and Travel Demand Forecasting: An Examination of the Scale Factor Problem', Transportation Research (25A), pp. 79-89

Wittink, D.R. and Montgomery, D.T. (1979), 'Predictive Validity of Trade-Off Analysis for Alternative Segmentation Schemes', Proceedings, American Marketing Association, Chicago, pp. 68-73

Chapter 5

Bates, J.J. and Roberts, M. (1986), 'Value of Time Research: Summary of Methodology and Findings', Proceedings of Seminar M, PTRC Summer Annual Meeting, Brighton

Benwell, M. and Black, I. (1985), 'User Valuation of Reliability in Inter-Urban Travel: Some Problems of Modelling and Measurement', Proceedings of Seminar L, PTRC 13th Summer Annual Meeting, July 1985

Crittle, F.J. and Johnson, L.W. (1980), 'Basic Logit (BLOGIT) Technical Manual', Australian Road Research Board Technical Manual ATM no.9, Victoria, Australia

Galvez-Perez, T.E. (1989), 'Assessment of Operating Policies in Public Transport: A Comprehensive Model Applied to a Rail Service, Ph.D. Thesis, University of Leeds (Commercial-in-Confidence)

Hensher, D.A. and Johnson, L. (1979), 'Applied Discrete Choice Modelling', Croom Helm

Jackson, W. and Jucker, J. (1981), 'An Empirical Study of Travel Time Variability and Travel Choice Behaviour, Transportation Science, vol. 16, no. 4

Knight, T.E. (1974), 'An Approach to the Evaluation of Changes in Travel Unreliability: A 'Safety Margin' Hypothesis', Transportation 3

MVA Consultancy, Institute for Transport Studies University of

Leeds, Transport Studies Unit University of Oxford (1987), 'The Value of Travel Time Savings', Policy Journals, Newbury, Berkshire

Sheldon, R.J. and Steer, J.K. (1982), 'The Use of Conjoint Analysis in Transportation Research, Proceedings of Seminar Q, PTRC Summer Annual Meeting, July 1982

Chapter 6

Ball, B. (1991), 'British Rail InterCity Strategic Planning', OR Insight, vol. 4, April, pp. 2-5

Bradley, M., Marks, P. and Wardman, M. (1986), 'A Summary of Four Studies into the Value of Travel Time Savings', paper to be presented at PTRC, 14th Summer Meeting, Seminar M

Central Statistical Office (1970), 'Social Trends 1970', no. 1, HMSO, London.

Chapman, R.G. and Staelin, R. (1982), 'Exploiting Rank Order Choice Set Data within the Stochastic Utility Model', Journal of Marketing Research, vol. XIX

Crittle, F.J. and Johnson, L.W. (1980), 'Basic Logit (BLOGIT) Technical Manual', Australian Road Research Board Technical Manual, no. 9

Department of Employment (1984), 'New Earnings Survey 1984', Government Statistical Office

Fowkes, A.S., Johnson, I. and Marks, P. (1985), 'Long Distance Business Travel and Mode Choice: The Results of Two Surveys of Business Travellers', Institute for Transport Studies, University of Leeds, Working Paper no. 211

Fowkes, A.S. and Marks, P. (1985), 'The Results of a Survey of Business Travel Policies in Greater London and North East England', Institute for Transport Studies, University of Leeds, Working Paper 202

Fowkes, A.S., Marks, P. and Nash, C.A. (1986), 'The Value of Business Travel Time Savings', Institute for Transport Studies,

University of Leeds, Working Paper 214.

Hensher, D.A. and Louviere, J.J. (1983), 'Identifying Individual Preferences for International Air Fares', Journal of Transport Economics and Policy, vol. XVII, no. 3

Judge, G.G., Hill, R.C., Griffiths, W.E., Lutkepohl, H. and Lee, T.C. (1982), 'Introduction to the Theory and Practice of Econometrics, John Wiley & Sons, 1982

Marks, P. (1986a), 'Long Distance Business Travel - A Literature Review', Institute for Transport Studies, University of Leeds, Technical Note 180

Marks, P. (1986b), 'Results from the Analysis of the Mode Choice Decisions of Long Distance Business Travellers', Institute for Transport Studies, University of Leeds, Working Paper 225

Marks, P., Fowkes, A.S. and Nash, C.A. (1986), 'Valuing Long Distance Business Travel Time Savings for Evaluation: A Methodological Review and Application', Transportation Planning Methods, Code P282, PTRC, London, pp. 87-98

MVA Consultancy; Institute for Transport Studies, University of Leeds and Transport Studies Unit, Oxford University (1987), 'The Value of Travel Time Savings - Policy Journals'

Royal Commission on the Distribution of Income and Wealth (1976), 'Report no. 3 Higher Incomes from Employment', Cmnd 6383, H.M.S.O., London

Steer, J., Davies and Gleave Ltd (1981), 'Elasticity of Demand in Respect of Service Frequency and Through Trains', report prepared for British Railways Board, 1981

TEST (1984), 'The Company Car Factor', A Report for the London Amenity and Transport Association, Transport and Environmental Studies, London

TRM Planning Partnership (1977), 'A Study of Business Values of Time', Final Report prepared for the Department of Transport, April 1977

University of Leeds (1971), 'InterCity Modal Split in Great Britain

Air v Rail', Centre for Transport Studies, University of Leeds

University of Southampton (1971), 'VTOL: A European Study (Potential Sites and Business Travel)', Volume Three: Business Travel, September 1971

Value of Time (1986), 'Research into the Value of Time', Final Report prepared for the Department of Transport by the MVA Consultancy, Institute for Transport Studies, University of Leeds and Transport Studies Unit, Oxford University

Wardman, M.R. (1986), 'Route Choice and the Value of Motorists' Time: Empirical Findings', Institute for Transport Studies, University of Leeds, Working Paper 224

Chapter 7

Frerk, M., Lindsay, I. and Fairhurst, M. (1981), 'Traffic Trends in the Seventies', London Transport Economic Research Report R428

Glaister, S. (1983), 'Some Characteristics of Rail Commute Demand', Journal of Transport Economics and Policy, vol. 17, no. 2

Greater London Council (1984), 'Central London Cordon Survey', 1982, Greater London Council

Hertfordshire County Council (1980), 'A Case Study on the role of Railway Modernisation in Suburban Development', Hertfordshire County Council Transport Coordination Unit

Mackett, R.L. (1983), 'The Leeds Integrated Land-Use Transport (LILT) Model', Department of Transport TRRL Supplementary Report SR805, Crowthorne: Transport and Road Research Laboratory

Mackett, R.L. (1984), 'The Impact of Transport Policy on the City', Department of Transport TRRL Supplementary Report SR821, Crowthorne: Transport and Road Research Laboratory

Mackett, R.L. (1985), 'Modelling the Impact of Rail Fare Increases', Transportation, vol. 12, pp. 293-312

Mackett, R.L. (1988), 'Modelling the Impact of Transport Cost Changes on Travel and Locational Behaviour', Department of Transport Working Paper WP(TP)62, Transport Planning Division, Safety and Transportation Group, Transport and Road Research Laboratory, Crowthorne

Mackett, R.L. (1989), 'Comparative Analysis of Modelling Land-Use Transport Interaction at the Micro and Macro Levels', Environment and Planning A, vol. 21

Mackett, R.L. (1990), 'Exploratory Analysis of Long-Term Travel Demand using Macro-Analytical Simulation', in New Developments in Dynamic and Activity Approaches to Travel Analysis (Jones, P. (ed)) pp. 384-405

Oldfield, R. and Tyler, E. (1981), 'The Elasticity of Medium Distance Rail Travel', TRRL Report LR993

Wardman, M. (1988), 'Comparison of RP and SP Models of Travel Behaviour', Journal of Transport Economics and Policy, vol. 22, no. 1

Chapter 8

Bates, J.J. (1988), 'Econometric Issues in Stated Preference Analysis', Journal of Transport Economics and Policy, vol. 22, no. 1, pp. 56-69

Bates, J.J., Ashley, D. and Hyman, G. (1987), 'The Nested Incremental Logit Model: Theory and Application to Modal Choice', PTRC Summer Annual Meeting, Seminar C, Bath

Bates, J.J. and Lowe, S.R. (1989), 'Criteria for Public Sector Support in Urban Public Transport', PTRC Summer Annual Meeting, Brighton

Benjamin, J. and Sen, L. (1982), 'Comparison of the Predictive Ability of Four Multi-attribute Approaches to Attitudinal Measurement', Transportation Research Record, no. 890, pp. 1-6

Black, W. and Black, T. (1982), 'Deriving Service Areas for Mass Transit Systems', Transportation Research, vol. 16A, no. 3, pp.

185-197

Clarke, A. (1988), 'The Use of New Local Rail Stations in West Yorkshire: A Re-appraisal', MA Dissertation, School of Economic Studies, University of Leeds

Couture, M. and Dooley, T. (1981), 'Analysing Traveler Attitudes to Resolve Intended and Actual Use of a New Transit Service', Transportation Research Record, no. 794, pp. 27-33

Crittle, F. and Johnson, L. (1980), 'Basic Logit (BLOGIT) Technical Manual', Australian Road Research Board, ATM no. 9, Vermont South, Victoria

Daly, A. (1987), 'Estimating Tree Logit Models', Transportation Research, vol. 21B, no. 4, pp. 251-268

Glaister, S. (1983), 'Some Characteristics of Rail Commuter Demand', Journal of Transport Economics and Policy vol. 17, no. 2, pp. 115-132

Heggie, I. and Papoulias, D. (1976), 'A Comparitive Evaluation of Forecast and Use of Park and Ride in Oxford', Traffic Engineering and Control, pp. 144-149

Hockenhull, G. (1984), 'Investigation of Demand for New Local Rail Stations in Leicestershire Examining Five Potential Sites', MSc Dissertation, Department of Civil Engineering, University of Leeds

Jones, I.S. and Nichols, A. (1983), 'The Demand for Inter City Rail Travel in the United Kingdom: Some Evidence', Journal of Transport Economics and Policy, vol. 17, no. 2, pp. 133-154

Koppelman, F. (1983), 'Predicting Transit Ridership in Response to Transit Service Changes', Journal of Transportation Engineering, vol. 109, pp. 548-564

Kumar, A. (1980), 'Use of Incremental Form of Logit Models in Demand Analysis', Transportation Research Record, no. 775, pp. 21-27

Louviere, J., Henley, D., Woodworth, G., Meyer, R., Levin, I., Stoner, J., Curry, D. and Anderson, D. (1981),

'Laboratory-Simulation versus Revealed-Preference Methods for Estimating Travel Demand Models', Transportation Research Record, no. 794, pp. 42-51

McFadden, D. (1979), 'Quantitative Methods for Analysing Travel Behaviour of Individuals: Some Recent Developments', In Hensher, D. and Stopher, P. (Eds) 'Behavioural Travel Modelling', Croom-Helm, London

McFadden, D. et al. (1979), 'Overview and Summary: Urban Travel Demand Forecasting Project', Research Report 796, Institute for Transportation Studies, University of California

MVA Consultancy, Institute for Transport Studies, University of Leeds and Transport Studies Unit, University of Oxford (1987), 'The Value of Travel Time Savings', Policy Journals, Newbury

Mason, K. and Preston, J. (1987), 'Leicester to Burton New Station Project: Interim Report on the Modelling Stage', Technical Note 213, Institute for Transport Studies, University of Leeds

Peakall, A.J. (1987), 'The Use of New Local Rail Stations in Freestanding Towns, M.A. Dissertation, Institute for Transport Studies, University of Leeds, unpublished

Preston, J. (1987), 'The Evaluation of New Local Rail Stations in West Yorkshire', Ph.D. Thesis, School of Economic Studies, University of Leeds

Preston, J. (1989), 'Nottingham - Mansfield - Worksop New Rail Service Project. Final Report', Institute for Transport Studies, University of Leeds, Unpublished

Preston, J. and Wardman, M. (1988), 'Demand Forecasting for New Local Rail Services: A Case Study of a New Service between Leicester and Burton on Trent', Working Paper 260, Institute for Transport Studies, University of Leeds

Preston, J. (1991), 'Comparing Alternative Demand Forecasting Techniques for New Local Rail Stations and Services', Journal of Transport Economics and Policy, 25A pp. 183-202

Railway Development Society (RDS) (1988), 'A-Z of Rail Re-Openings', RDS, Great Bookham

Ruhl, A., Daly, A. and Dobson, G. (1979), 'The Use of Disaggregate Models for Railway Investment Decisions in Holland', PTRC Summer Annual Meeting, Seminar M, Warwick

Sheldon, R. and Steer, J. (1982), 'The Use of Conjoint Analysis in Transport Research', PTRC Summer Annual Meeting, Seminar Q, Warwick

Stark, D. (1981), 'Time Series Analysis of Glagow Suburban Rail Patronage', Supplementary Report 649, TRRL, Crowthorne

Tyler, J. and Hassard, R. (1973), 'Gravity/Elasticity Models for the Planning of the Inter Urban Rail Passenger Business', PTRC Summer Annual Meeting, Brighton

Westin, R. (1974), 'Predictions from Binary Choice Models', Journal of Econometrics, vol. 2, no. 1, pp. 1-16

West Midlands County Council (with the assistance of the MVA Consultancy) (1984), 'West Midlands Rail Mode Choice Models', Joint Transport Planning Unit

White, P and Williams, S. (1976), 'Modelling Cross Country Rail Passenger Trips', PTRC Summer Annual Meeting, Seminar N, Warwick

Whitehead, P. (1981), 'Estimating the Effects on Revenue of Rail Service Changes', PTRC Summer Annual Meeting, Seminar K, Warwick

Chapter 9

Downes, J.D. and Gynenes, L. (1976), 'Temporal Stability and Forecasting Ability of Trip Generation Models in Reading', Transport and Road Research Laboratory Report 726, Department of the Environment, Crowthorne, Berkshire

Hill, E.C., Rickard, J.M., Nash, C.A. and Fowkes, A.S. (1989), 'The Effects of Demographic Change on British Rail's Long-Distance Passenger Market', final report to British Rail, Institute for Transport Studies, University of Leeds

Kendall, M.G. and Stuart, A. (1958), 'Advanced Theory of Statistics',

Griffin, London

McCullagh, P. and Nelder, J.A. (1983), 'Generalised Linear Models', Monographs in Statistics and Applied Probability: Series Editors Cox, D.R. and Hinkley, D.V., Chapman and Hall, London

Rickard, J.M. (1986), 'Modelling of the Factors Influencing Long-Distance Rail Passenger Trip Rates in Great Britain', unpublished PhD Thesis, School of Economic Studies, University of Leeds

Rickard, J.M. (1988), 'Factors Influencing Long-Distance Rail Passenger Trip Rates in Great Britain', Journal of Transport Economics and Policy, XXII (2), pp. 209-234

Rickard, J.M., Fowkes, A.S. and Nash, C.A. (1987), 'Applications of Long-Distance Trip Generation Models', Institute for Transport Studies, Technical Note 207, unpublished, University of Leeds

Stopher, P.R. and Meyburg, A.H. (1975), 'Urban Transportation Modelling and Planning', Lexington Books